THE EMMA GOLDMAN TRILOGY

THE EMMA GOLDMAN TRILOGY

Three Plays About the Most Dangerous Woman in America

JESSICA LITWAK

The Emma Goldman Trilogy, Copyright © 2020 Jessica Litwak
CAUTION: Professionals and amateurs are hereby warned that *THE EMMA GOLDMAN TRILOGY* is subject to a royalty. It is fully protected under the copyright laws of the United States of America, Dominion of Canada, United Kingdom, and all British Commonwealth countries, and all countries covered by the International Copyright Union, the Pan-American Copyright Convention, the Universal Copyright Convention, the Berne Convention, and of all countries with which the United States of America has reciprocal copyright relations. All rights, including professional/ amateur stage rights, motion picture, recitation, lecturing, public reading, radio broadcasting, television, video or sound taping, video or sound recording, all other forms of mechanical or electronic reproduction, such as CD-ROM, CD-I, DVD, information storage and retrieval systems and photocopying, and rights of translation into foreign languages, are strictly reserved. Particular emphasis is placed upon the matter of readings, permission for which must be secured from the Author's agent in writing. All inquiries concerning rights should be addressed to: Susan Schulman of Susan Schulman Literary Agency, 454 West 44th Street, New York, NY 10036, or emailed to Susan Schulman at susan@schulmanagency.com. No professional performance of the Play may be given without obtaining in advance the written permission of Susan Schulman Literary Agency, and paying the requisite fee

All rights are strictly reserved. No part of this book may be reproduced in any form or by any electronic or mechanical means, including information storage and retrieval systems, without permission in writing from the Author's agent, except by a reviewer, who may quote brief passages in a review. Any members of educational institutions wishing to photocopy part or all of the work for classroom use, or publishers who would like to obtain permission to include the work in an anthology, should send their inquires to: Susan Schulman of Susan Schulman Literary Agency, 454 West 44th Street, New York, NY 10036, or email Susan Schulman at susan@schulmanagency.com.

Special Notice:
Anyone receiving permission to produce *THE EMMA GOLDMAN TRILOGY* is required to give credit to the Author as sole and exclusive Author of the Play on the title page of all programs distributed in connection with performances of the Play and in all instances in which the title of the Play appears for purposes of advertising, publicizing or otherwise exploiting the Play and/or production thereof. The name of the Author must appear on a separate line, on which no other name appears, immediately beneath the title and in size of type equal to 50% of the size of the largest, most prominent letter used for the title of the Play. No person, firm, or entity may receive credit larger or more prominent than that accorded the Author.

Table of Contents

Jessica Litwak vii
Author's Note: xi

Emma Goldman, Love, Anarchy and Other Affairs 1
The Snake and The Falcon 32
Nobody is Sleeping 97

Jessica Litwak

Jessica Litwak is a playwright, actor, drama therapist, director, puppet builder and recognized leader in the field of socially engaged theatre.

Her plays have been produced Off Broadway and on stages across the U.S., Europe and the U.K. including The Goodman Theatre, Rattlestick Theatre, Archa Theatre, The Women's Project, La MaMa, DR2, The Renberg Theatre, and The Edinburgh Festival. Plays include: _Dream Acts_, _A Pirate's Lullaby_, _The Promised Land_, _Secret Agents_, _I Won't Be Afraid_, _The Narcissism of Small Differences_, _Victory Dance_, _The Night It Rained_, _Terrible Virtue_, _Wider Than The Sky_ _My Heart is in the East_, _The Wall_, _Sometimes the Lights_, _Reincarnation_ and _50,000 Mice_." As a playwright and cultural critic, Litwak is published by No Passport Press, TCG, Applause Books, Smith and Krause, and The New York Times, Drama Therapy Review, Engaged Scholar Journal, HowlRound, and TCG Salon.

As an actress Litwak has performed on stages across the U.S. and in Europe, she has appeared in film, television and radio. She wrote and directed _The Fear Project_ funded by the U.S. State Department in the Czech Republic as well as at the Sabhagar Theatre Festival in Kolkata, India. She directed her play _The Moons Of Jupiter_ at Naropa University in Colorado. She directed _What Would You Name Her?_ at The Citizen's Theatre in Glasgow.

In 2005 Litwak founded the New Generation Theatre Ensemble where she built training and performance opportunities for youth, and directed her plays for youth: _GRIM, Postcards from Canterbury, The Great Journey Home, Verona High,_ and _War: An American Dream._

In 2010 Litwak founded the H.E.A.T. Collective (www.the-heatcollective.org) in order to coalesce her practice and workshops, events, and productions that bring together the practices of Healing, Education, and Activism through Theatre. She serves as Artistic Director.

In the days following the 2016 election, she founded Artists Rise Up New York, designed to create free theatre actions in response to the needs of community. ARUNY produced five theatrical events, engaging audiences and building community. She has also worked extensively with Artists Rise Up Los Angeles.

Litwak is a graduate of RADA, NYU, Columbia University and Antioch University with a BFA in acting, an MFA in playwriting and a Ph.D. in Theatre as Leadership and Change. She has served as faculty at institutions such as Columbia, NYU, Lesley University, Whitman College, Hollins, Naropa, The Theatre Academy at Los Angeles City College, Marymount, Stella Adler Academy. Internationally, she has regularly taught at Masaryk University (Czech Republic) and the International Director's Symposium at La Mama Umbria (Italy). Her workshops are frequently hosted by The Freedom Theatre and Yes Theatre in Palestine. She has conducted seminars for international bodies such as The Global Mobility Symposium and The World Economic Forum, the North American Drama Therapy Association, The International Leadership Association, The International Peace and Research Association, and has served as an arts curator for The European City of Culture campaign. She conducts ongoing theatre and drama therapy workshops at domestic violence shelters, prisons and a facility for formerly incarcerated women. Her Puppets for the People workshop is featured in conferences and at universities, and theatre companies around the globe.

She is a core member of Theatre Without Borders. She is a Fulbright Scholar.

The Emma Goldman Trilogy has been produced and supported by The Women's Project, The Lark, Brava for Women in the Arts, Serious Play, Theatre Lab, La MaMa, The Arlene Francis Center, and The Bay Area Women's Theatre Festival.

Author's Note:

Long ago Anne Bogart cast me in a big play called <u>History, an American Dream</u>. It was performed at St. Marks Church and there were what seemed like hundreds of dancers on the floor below, while a handful of historical characters gave speeches from the balcony. I remember Eugene Victor Debs, Douglas MacArthur, and Jane Adams, Anita Bryant among others. Bogart told me: "you are going to be Emma Goldman". I looked at her blankly: "Who is that?" Despite the fact that my Aunt had grown up in an Anarchist commune and known Emma Goldman as a child, and despite the fact that Goldman was part of my heritage as the granddaughter of Russian Jewish radicals, I had never heard of her. Bogart handed me a copy of Goldman's autobiography Living My Life. "Read" she said. And I read.

I was 24 years old. I discovered that at my age Emma was just as neurotic and vulnerable as I was. She was worried about the size of her hips, the way she appeared in a particular hat, and whether a certain man or woman found her attractive. Yet, despite her trivial humanness, she had also been in prison more than once by my age, arrested and incarcerated for defending her ideals. While reading her autobiography, I realized that a person does not need to be born brave, with inherited superpowers, in fact a person can be rather silly, often terrified, self-doubting, full of flaws, and still able to make courageous choices and do heroic things. A light bulb went off in my heart. I now knew how to imagine the rest of my life. The directive was two words long: Be Brave. I kept an anagram in my pocket. I would pull it out and look at it when I was diagnosed with cancer, when I was going through divorces, or two long births, when my oldest daughter (Emma's namesake) was diagnosed with a brain tumor. The note read: WWED? What would Emma Do?

After History, An American Dream was over, Anne Bogart and I decided to make a one woman play about Emma Goldman. We walked into the studio the first day and Anne asked me to come up with 90 things Emma believed in. From that came the long poem that still exists at the end of Love, Anarchy and Other Affairs.

When I researched the first play I had the great privilege of meeting and speaking with an anarchist friend of my Aunt's, Arne Thorne. Thorne had been with Emma at the front at The Spanish Civil War. He was with her when she had her final stroke and witnessed her surprising modesty and grace at her most vulnerable moment, a moment I have written into Nobody is Sleeping.

We raised money for that first play with a party called Night of Anarchy: A Big Dance. All our friends' bands played. Anne and I auditioned for Julia Miles for the Women's Project and Productions. The only space available in the theatre that day was Tammy Grimes' dressing room, so we crowded in and did the whole thing right there, crew and all. Julia got the idea that day for a festival of one woman plays about Women Heroes. It became an Off Broadway show and a collection of short plays about women heroes produced by The Women's Project and Productions.

Next I tackled the subject of Emma's deportation in her fiftieth year. The Snake and Falcon came out of extensive research and an explorative rehearsal process that resulted in several sets of staged readings: the first one performed in an Off Broadway theatre where the air conditioning was broken. It was 103 degrees that night. We sustained our courageous audience with Gin Daisies, a favorite pre prohibition cocktail in 1919, the year the play takes place.

The first two plays were presented in staged reading at Theatre J in Washington D.C., Ari Roth had an idea during the talkbacks for the plays. He dared me to write a third play, to create an Emma Goldman marathon. To write Nobody Is Sleeping I traveled to Spain to research The Spanish Civil War. My experiences in

Spain included my daughter Emma (named for Goldman) getting detained by police when we were trying to find Durruti's grave in a Spanish cemetery and me getting chased by guards after spitting on Franco's tomb.

I have spent over three decades researching and writing about Goldman, a dedicated "Emmasary" of The Emma Goldman Papers, I spent much of my artistic life invested in telling E.G.'s story, while supporting Emma's legacy of freedom and social justice. I have named my oldest daughter after her. I have marched in her footsteps and tried to live up to her integrity and courage, while reaching for a semblance of her intelligence and wit.

The three plays in this trilogy cover four decades of Goldman's life. The trilogy begins with a one woman play: Love, Anarchy and Other Affairs – one actor, one night in 1901 when Emma is hiding in a Chicago apartment just before she is arrested for her alleged complicity in the assassination of President McKinley. The Snake and The Falcon, the second play in the trilogy, told by four or five actors, takes place during six months in 1919 when Emma was pitted against the young zealous J. Edgar Hoover who dubs her "the most dangerous woman in America" and deports her to Russia. This play deals with immigration laws that have changed very little in the last hundred years. The trilogy culminates with Nobody Is Sleeping, an ensemble play about the Spanish Civil War. The cast creates the revolution itself. Although the facts of the war itself are tragic (Franco declared a victorious end to the Spanish Civil War in Spain just months before Hitler invaded Poland and World War Two began) The spirit of this third play is as wild and multi-layered as the revolution it depicts. The many characters that help evoke this exciting personal and political story include Franco (as a puppeteer manipulating Hitler, Stalin, FDR, Chamberlain among many others), Durruti, Lorca, Ernest Hemingway, and of course Alexander Berkman and Emma Goldman. My daughter Emma Weinstein helped me build Franco's puppets, which are shot, hung, tortured, coerced and decapitated. The play evokes this chaotic, beautiful, and unique period in history.

The three plays together give the audience a full experience of Emma's life and work. The relationship with her lifelong comrade Alexander Berkman runs through all three plays, one of the most unusual love stories of all time

The scripts had each performed alone, but my dream was to perform them together. This has come to kind of fruition with The Emma Goldman Day Happening in honor of Women's History Month done in March 2016, 2017, and 2019 in New York and California at La MaMa, Theatre Lab and The Arlene Francis Cneter. The plays interspersed with discussions led by panels of people who have knowledge about the subjects covered in the plays. There is also a specific meal between each play which reflects the time and place of the dramaturgy. It is a very special interactive theatrical happening.

One sample schedule was:

> The Emma Goldman Trilogy Happening
> 2:00 Welcoming Circle
> 2:30 Love, Anarchy and Other Affairs
> 4:00 Panel Discussion: Anarchy, Activism, Women's Rights, Political Prisoners, etc.
> Audience is served Tea and Russian Cookies.
> 5:00 The Snake and The Falcon
> 6:30 Panel Discussion: Immigration, Deportation, Reproductive Rights, etc.
> Audience is served Sandwiches and Russian Vodka
> 7:30 Nobody is Sleeping
> 9:00 Panel Discussion: Revolution, Movements, History as Change Agent, etc.
> Audience is served Red Wine and Tapas.
> 10:00 Closing Circle

These successful events convinced me of the vitality of doing these plays as a trilogy. The community that grew around the plays and the discussions and the shared food – was vibrant and empowering. The balance between art and action, between history and present tense, enabled us to see the issues in our current world with insight, humor and ferocity, knowing that we have both the motivation and the means to inspire and initiate change.

I am grateful to so many people who have put their hearts and energy into this work. There are too many people to mention, the directors and actors who have brought the play to life at various times, as well as the wonderful stalwart folks at The Emma Goldman Papers in Berkeley who believe in who Emma was and who we all can still be in her memory.

I am grateful for the support The Emma Goldman Trilogy has received from The Women's Project, The Lark, Brava for Women in the Arts, Serious Play, Theatre Lab, La MaMa, The Arlene Francis Center, and The Bay Area Women's Theatre Festival.

These plays are dedicated to all you Emmasaries out there who keep Emma's memory alive with thoughts, speech and actions of justice and freedom, and to Emma Goldman – I hope she would approve of my vision of her. And to my daughters Emma and Sophie who are to me what Sasha was to Emma Goldman: my inspiration and my home.

Emma Goldman, Love, Anarchy and Other Affairs

By Jessica Litwak

CHARACTERS:
EMMA GOLDMAN
MAN's VOICE
SASHA* Sasha can appear at the end if the play is done as part of the *Emma Goldman Trilogy*, if the play is produced as a stand-alone piece, his appearance here is not necessary.

SETTING: One room of a tenement apartment in Chicago, September 9th, 1901.

There is a chair, a trunk (that becomes Emma's public speaking platform), and a small table with a bowl, a glass and a pitcher of water. There is a cot (that becomes various beds and Sasha's prison cell), piles of books everywhere and a table with an oil lamp. There is some indication that the inhabitants of the room left in a hurry. Slides and music are optional.

As the audience enters there is a slide projected onto one wall. "Anarchism: The philosophy of a new social order based on liberty unrestricted by man-made law."

As the house lights dim, the slide changes to a newspaper clipping from September 1901 describing the assassination of President McKinley. A Man's Voice is heard (pre-recorded or live, he has the sound of a an early 20th century news announcer).

During his speech we hear a knocking.

MAN'S VOICE: CITIZENS, BEWARE. A treacherous anarchist is at large. A warrant has been issued for the immediate capture and arrest of EMMA GOLDMAN, a suspect in the brutal assassination of President William McKinley.
EMMA: Max?... Max? Are you there?
MAN'S VOICE: If you see EMMA GOLDMAN or know of her whereabouts notify your local authorities at once.

A door opens and Emma enters the room in the dark. She feels her way around the room. His speech overlaps her actions.

MAN'S VOICE: On September 6th, in Buffalo, New York, William McKinley was shot. The gunman was quickly apprehended. His name is Leon Czlosgoz and he confessed to being an ANARCHIST who was influenced by EMMA GOLDMAN. He has stated that the writings and lectures of EMMA GOLDMAN incited him to commit this act of violence against the President of the United States.

A recording of Emma's voice.

EMMA'S VOICE: Anarchism will it lead to revolution? Indeed it will. No real social change has ever come about without revolution. Anarchism is the theory of social harmony that is reconstructing the world, and that will usher in the dawn.

Emma crashes into something

EMMA: Oy.
MAN'S VOICE: Vice President Roosevelt has stated that America will take action to stamp out anarchy all together. A nationwide search for EMMA GOLDMAN is underway.

Lights come up on Emma Goldman as she turns on a lamp she is wearing a coat and a little hat with withered flowers. Emma sees the audience.

EMMA: Men! Meshugguh! Max! He wires to me: "Emma, if you must come to Chicago, at least you'll stay by me. You'll be safe. I gotta lotta locks on the door." A lotta locks? It's wide open! And where's Max? Oy. I don't like to think about it.

MAN'S VOICE: Two hundred detectives have been sent throughout the country to track this treacherous criminal down.

EMMA: The silliest thing just happened. I was sneaking through the crowds, and all of the sudden I realize that I was holding my bag to my face. To protect it. So that if I am unexpectedly attacked, beaten and killed, my face would remain unharmed. No scars. Such feminine vanity... what would Sasha say?

MAN'S VOICE: EMMA GOLDMAN is believed to be in the vicinity of Chicago. Homes of several anarchists have been raided and men and women known to be friendly with EMMA GOLDMAN have been arrested and charged with conspiracy. Until the authorities can locate Emma Goldman. until EMMA GOLDMAN is found.

EMMA: I am... Smith. E.G. Smith. At least that's the name I've been using recently.

MAN'S VOICE: DO NOT, I repeat, DO NOT approach EMMA GOLDMAN or attempt to detain her. She may be armed and is extremely DANGEROUS.

EMMA: At the train station there were a lot of men in gray suits. Detectives. Looking for me. A large nasty-looking criminal. I slipped past them in my little brown hat. They were watching everyone who got off the train. Standing in corners. Leaning against walls. Pretending to read newspapers. Taking notes. Making secret little gestures at each other. Such professionals. They think you can't tell them apart from the rest of the general public. They think they're invisible, the authorities. But I know a police officer when I see one!

Emma takes off her hat and coat.

EMMA: Tonight I intend to relax. Relax? I have just been accused of conspiring to assassinate the President of the United States. Relax? All over the streets they are saying: "Anarchists should be exterminated. Their tongues cut out, their carcasses EMMA (CONT'D): soaked in oil and burnt alive." Just this afternoon I was riding the train with a charming young lady. She was wearing one of those new hats. It was blue and there were pears and flowers bouncing about to one side. It was very becoming. She turned to me and said, "Have you read the morning papers? This Emma Goldman is a beast, a bloodthirsty monster, she should have been locked up long ago." "Locked up nothing," said the gentleman sitting behind us. "She should have her heart cut out and fed to my dog!" I am nodding politely. After all, what do I know of Emma Goldman? I'm Smith. Just plain old E.G.

Emma hangs up her hat on a hook on the wall. Music comes on: Wagner. She turns downstage and imagines newspaper headlines suspended in air.

EMMA: ASSASSIN OF PRESIDENT MCKINLEY AN ANARCHIST. SAID TO HAVE BEEN INCITED BY EMMA GOLDMAN. WOMAN ANARCHIST WANTED. Did I incite him? I don't remember. I only met him one time. We spoke for half an hour. This poor boy. I wonder what drove him to do this terrible thing. It is reported that he said, "I did it for the working people." Well. Sasha also did something once for the working people. The people are asleep. They are indifferent and afraid.

Music off. Emma takes off her coat and hangs it up.

EMMA: I promised Max I would escape to Canada in the morning. He said I'm crazy to come here. "The police are everywhere, Emma. Hungry for your blood." I am not afraid of prison. After all Sasha is in prison, he has been in prison now for ten years... I don't like to think about it.

She peeks in the bathroom behind a screen or curtain.

EMMA: Hey! Maybe I should make a bubble bath! In the old country in the midst of the Cossacks, and the pogroms and my father's temper, my mother used to make us take a warm bath. "Remember, Emma, there's nothing like hot water to calm the nerves." Yes, a bath could be useful.

She disappears into the bathroom and then immediately reappears again.

EMMA : But then of course you're naked, and more vulnerable to surprise...You know what Max said? He said if the police would come here tonight, he would tell them I am the maid. The maid? Isn't that what they called Joan of Arc? Remember what happened to her? I don't like to think about it.

Emma picks up the letters

EMMA: Sasha, tonight I have to destroy your precious letters so no more names will be linked with mine. I don't like to think about it.

She looks up at the audience

How about I tell a story? Just to pass the time till our elusive host returns. The tale of how I came to be a "bloodthirsty monster." Where shall we begin? It's now September 1901. In Chicago, America. And I am hiding...No! I am waiting...No! I am

RELAXING at Max's house. And I will tell you a little story. It's my story. A love story.

> *Blackout. Music. During the next speech, a series of slides appears on the wall or screen: images of Emma, other immigrants, workers and revolutionaries and images of turn-of-the-century America.*

Emma Goldman was born in Kovno, Lithuania on June 27th, 1869. She grew up in Russia and came to America in 1885 at the age of sixteen. She lived with her father and her sister in Rochester, New York. She worked in a factory making two dollars and fifty cents a week. In 1886 Emma Goldman married Jacob Kirshner-an immigrant who worked at the machine next to hers at Garson's Clothing Works. In America, Labor strikes were breaking out. The working people were demanding an eight-hour day. On May 4th, 1887, a mass meeting of workers was called in Chicago's Haymarket Square. The crowd addressed by five anarchist speakers. It was a quiet and orderly meeting until the police burst in and began beating people with clubs. A bomb sailed through the air, exploding, killing a couple of policemen. All five of the anarchist speakers were arrested...

> *Music off. Slides off. Lights up. Emma takes her glasses off.*

My father's name was Abraham. Abraham Goldman. He did not think of himself as a drinking man. He only drank on special occasions. You know, holidays. Jewish holidays. National holidays. Saturdays. Sundays. Schnapps. Glass after glass after glass. The more he drank the angrier he got. He would look around the room for something to spark his fury.. For some reason, his eyes would always land on me.

"WHO IS THAT DIRTY KID? SHE AIN'T MINE. SHE DON'T EVEN LOOK LIKE ME. WHERE DID SHE COME FROM, THE GARBAGE PAIL? SHE AIN'T EVEN PRETTY. SHE'S LOUD-MOUTHED. DISRESPECTFUL. HER HAIR IS A MESS. SHE

AIN'T EVEN A GIRL, SHE'S A PIG! GET OUT OF HERE YOU UGLY BRAT BEFORE I BEAT YOU TO DEATH!"

He is very big. He hits so hard my screams wake up the whole neighborhood. My sister Helena tries to stop him. He keeps striking me. She bites him on the leg. He shouts, falls down. She carries me to her room and locks the door.

When I am old enough my father can't wait to marry me off. He is happy with Jacob. Jacob is exactly like my father. They are a match made in heaven.

My father and Jacob believe that women should be submissive, subdued. They look pretty, bear children and cook delicious soups. My father and Jacob do not approve of women being involved in political activity of any kind. So, Helena and I have to sneak out of the house.

We have become interested in the trial of the Haymarket Anarchists from Chicago. We attend regular meetings in Rochester to discuss the trial with young people like ourselves. My father and Jacob get word of this. They are angry but they dismiss our actions as the passing obsession of foolish girls… until one particular afternoon.

Not too many people can pinpoint the precise moment in history when they discovered their life's purpose. November 11, 1887. Black Friday.

Helena and I are walking back from the meeting. We have just heard the news. Four of the brave anarchists have been hung. Another has committed suicide in his cell. Helena is crying. I am in shock.

Emma steps forward. Lights shift.

I woke up early. My head was clear for the first time.

Emma steps back, Lights shift.

I am in my father's kitchen. Jacob is there. And others. Everyone is talking about the news from Chicago. I am staring at the teakettle.

I know they were innocent. Five of them dead. Arrested and hung. I feel sick

Emma steps forward. Lights shift.

I woke up early. My head was clear for the first time. I had the distinct sensation that something new and wonderful had happened to me.

Emma steps back. Lights shift.

I am in the kitchen. My father's loud voice from across the room. "Those anarchists were murderers. They deserve to be hung." I look up at him, "What did you say?" "Shut up, girl. No one is talking to you." Suddenly something snaps in me. One leap and I'm at his throat. "Get out. Get out or I will kill you." They pull me back. "The child's gone crazy." I pick up a pitcher of water and throw it in his face.

Emma steps forward.

I woke up early. My head was clear for the first time. I had the distinct sensation that something new and wonderful had happened to me. I had an ideal. A reason for living.

Emma steps back. Lights shift.

My father is hitting me. "YOU ARE A DISGRACE." My mother is hiding. Helena is weeping. Jacob is drinking Schnapps. My father's voice filling the kitchen. His hands slapping. I look up at him. Five of them dead. Arrested and hung. "I hate you, Father." His fingers close into a fist. I black out. The next morning...

Emma steps forward. Lights shift.

I woke up early. My head was clear for the first time. I had the distinct sensation that something new and wonderful had happened to me. I had an ideal. A reason for living. I decide to leave my husband and my father and devote my life to freedom. I am a grown woman. I am an anarchist.

Lights shift. Emma hears a noise and rushes over to check the door and the window. She is frightened, but nobody is there. She returns to her chair.

August 15th, 1889. The day I met Alexander Berkman. I arrive in New York City. I have the address of an aunt, five dollars, and one small handbag. It is Sunday. Very hot. I am asking directions. I walk all the way from Forty-Second Street to the Bowery, a tenement five floors up. My aunt and her family crowded into two small rooms. They seem surprised to see me.

"Emma, why have you come to New York?"

"Emma, did you really leave your husband?"

"Emma, how do you intend to make a living?"

"Emma, do you realize how hard it is for a woman alone?"

Their voices make me...sleepy. They sound like flies buzzing. I have left everything behind me to start a new life. This interrogation is very upsetting. I'm going out for a little walk, I tell them. A walk? It's 95 degrees out there. I wander around New York City... On Third Street I meet a man I have seen in Rochester. He takes me to Sach's Cafe, a gathering place for artists and revolutionaries and workers. We sit down at a table and I hear a loud voice: "Bring me an extra-large steak. An extra-large cup of coffee!" "Who is that glutton?" I ask. "That is Alexander Berkman. He never has much money, but when he does he eats Sach's right out of food. He's a very serious young anarchist. One of those obsessive types. The cause above all else, you know the kind. Shall I introduce him to you?" I approach the table. He stands up to shake my hand.

"Alexander Berkman, Emma Goldman."

He is a boy of eighteen, but with the neck and chest of a giant. Big shoulders. Strong arms. Beautiful brown eyes. Soft lips. Very severe forehead. Somehow a little frightening. We look at each other. I am smiling. I don't know why. "Hello." Very nervous. "Pleased to meet you." I reach out to shake his hand. I stumble over the leg of the table and he catches me up in his arms. "I saved your life," he says. "Well I certainly hope that someday I will have the opportunity of saving yours."

It was two weeks after that, when he was taking me to Brooklyn to meet Johann Most…we were riding the elevated. That is the day I began to tell Alexander Berkman all about myself. He interrupted me. "Call me Sasha," he said. Sasha…

September 1889. Johann Most was a prominent anarchist. He published an anarchist newspaper called The Freiheit. It was Johann Most who convinced me to begin public speaking. I was never so terrified of anything in my life. I'd get up to speak at a meeting and when I'd open my mouth, no words would come out, just a kind of gasping for air like a fish. My face would get hot and turn red and I would begin perspiring. This was very embarrassing, but Johann Most believed in my passion. He did not have much regard for the revolutionary seal of most women; he referred to them as "emotional stupids." But I guess he thought I was different.

He said he wanted to make me a great speaker to take his place after he was gone. He'd take me out to dinner, and we'd drink a lot of wine and he's laugh and toast, "To your first public speech, little Emma." We'd go to expensive places and he'd order wonderful things and buy me flowers afterwards. This made Sasha very mad. Sasha said Most had no right to spend money on me when the movement was in so much need of it. Sasha said that it was inconsistent for an anarchist to enjoy luxuries when The People live in poverty. But I had a hard time criticizing Johann Most for anything he did. He was my idol. He was the best public speaker I ever heard. He could turn a whole room to flame with the furious clarity of his voice. I worshipped him, and he…loved me.

Once he grabbed me in a cab and kissed me all over my face and…arms. He was incredibly ugly, but I let him do it because he was such a great man and I wanted to make him happy. It is amazing to me that just a few years after he got me started on my way he turned against us.

Lights shift. Soft music

1890. Sasha. The meeting is over. Sasha and I file out with the others. We walk all the way home in silence. When we get to the house where I live, my whole body begins to shake. Like a fever. I look at Sasha. He comes upstairs. I have a very narrow bed. We are squished together in the darkness. He whispers soft Russian words into my ear, which makes me drowsy... I begin to drift into a dreamy sleep... then suddenly there is an electric current rushing through me... a soft, shy hand... trembling, touching me tenderly. I reach out for the hand; we are in a wild embrace. Then a beautiful pain pierces through everything that has been dormant, unconscious, suppressed. In the morning I am still reaching out, eagerly, hungrily seeking. He is sleeping, now. I gaze at this boy that attracts me and repels me all at the same time. He is so hard and yet so tender. I kiss his thick black hair and then I fall asleep beside him.

Lights shift. Loud music. Emma begins to dance.

We are at a dance. I love dancing. I'm the wildest dancer in the room. I won't come off the floor. I see Sasha's cousin coming towards me... grab his arms and give him a spin... he pulls away from me... his face is very serious, as if he's about to announce the death of a beloved comrade or something. "Emma, an anarchist should not be dancing so recklessly, with such abandon. You are on your way to becoming a force in the movement. It is undignified." "Undignified? Who the hell are you? To throw the cause up in my face when I'm having such a wonderful time? How can a cause that stands for such a beautiful ideal—for freedom from convention and prejudice—demand the denial of joy? Do you want me to become a nun with the cause as my cloister? No, I want to dance... and if I can't dance, I don't want to be a part of your revolution."

People are staring at me. My voice is too loud. Some people are clapping, but others are shouting. I look for Sasha's face in the crowd. He is furious with me. I know what he is thinking. He's thinking one must love the cause above all else. He is thinking I am selfish and silly and immature. But I know what I feel, Sasha. I know what I believe. He turns and walks out of the hall.

I am alone.

Lights shift. Emma sits in the chair and rolls a cigarette.

I had other lovers. One of them way Fedya-Sasha's best friend. Fedya was a painter. One day he asked me to pose naked for him. So I did. In the middle of the painting he had to stop. He said he was too nervous. We became lovers. When Sasha came home, I told him, and the two men embraced. That night the three of us stayed up talking-we made a pact: to dedicate ourselves to the cause—to live for our ideals and to die together if necessary…

Lights shift. Emma stands.

May 1892.

Emma becomes a young woman of twenty-three.

Sasha is upstairs building a bomb. He's never done it before, but we have a copy of The Science of Revolutionary Warfare, and it gives us a pretty good description.

Slides come on: a series of photographs of workers being oppressed and beaten, ending with a picture of Henry Clay Frick.

Henry Clay Frick. Big Boss. Carnegie Steel Mills. Wages cut. Workers strike. Mills are closed. Workers attacked. Beaten and killed. Henry Clay Frick. Infamous piece of scum.

Slides out. Lights shift.

Sasha decides to kill him. Sasha got some dynamite from a man on Staten Island. Sasha says: "I have waited all my life for the sublime moment to serve the cause. To give my life for the people."

Sasha says although he will live long enough to justify his act in court, he knows he will be condemned to death. "I have waited all my life for the sublime moment to serve the cause. To give my life..."

Oh Sasha. The more you talk, the sicker I feel, I am oblivious to everything: Cause, Duty, Message... what do these things mean compared with the force of our love? Do our three years together mean so little to you that you can sit up there calmly expecting me to go on living after you've been blown to bits or strangled to death?

I will go with you, Sasha. I can help. Besides, I simply must go with you, don't you understand? An argument ensues.

Finally he agrees to let me go with him, at least as far as Pittsburgh.

On the train.

Emma, waiting for Sasha to build the bomb, falls asleep on the floor. She wakes up suddenly. Some time has passed.

The bomb didn't go off... and if the test bomb doesn't go off, that means the second bomb made out of the same materials won't go off either. We have lost thirty dollars and a week of our time. Now I'll never be able to go with Sasha; we don't have enough money for train fares. Now we have to raise the money to buy a gun. I told Sasha, "I'll take care of it!" So... how does one go about raising quick cash? How does a woman, alone in New York City, go about raising a large amount of cash quickly?

How far does one go for the man one loves? For the cause?

Well, I got the idea from Dostoyevsky. In Crime and Punishment, Sonia became a prostitute to support her little brother and sister, and when the men came, she lay on her cot with her shoulders twitching and her face to the wall. If sensitive Sonia could sell her body, then certainly I can... The question is, am I attractive enough for the men on the streets? I look tired. But my complexion is good. I have nice hair. I'm a little too large in the hips for my age, but I'm a Jew, from the old country, I look like my grandmother, it's something to be proud of! Besides, I could always wear a corset and high heels... Oy.

July 16th, 1892.

I am walking up and down Fourteenth Street. I join the long procession of girls I have seen so often. I try to mimic their calm. They disappear into doorways with men and then reappear again. Every time a man comes by me, I get nauseous, and then I panic as he passes me by: I have to raise the money to buy a gun! It's 11 o'clock and still I've had no luck. Finally, an elderly man in a pinstripe suit approaches me. He beckons me to follow him into a barroom. He orders two glasses of wine. "I don't know what drove you to the streets, but I'm sure it wasn't looseness, or lack of excitement in your personal life." "Many girls are driven to it by economic necessity," I tell him. "I'm not interested in economic necessity, or in the reason you were out there, I'll just tell you one thing: There's nothing in prostitution unless you have a knack for it. And you most certainly... do not." He puts a ten-dollar bill down on the table. "Now go home," he says. "Don't you want me to do something? Take off my clothes or something?" "You are a sweet kid," he says, "but you are silly and stupid and immature." "I was twenty-three last month!" He laughs at me, and I run all the way home. With ten dollars for the gun.

Lights shift.

July 23rd. Saturday.

YOUNG MAN BY THE NAME OF ALEXANDER BERKMAN SHOOTS FRICK. ASSASSIN OVERPOWERED BY WORKING MEN AFTER DESPERATE STRUGGLE.

I ran after the departing train. We only had money for one ticket. He said only one person was needed for the job. He barged into Frick's office and shot the bastard three times. In the neck, in the shoulder.

There was blood. Men ran in. They took the gun. He had a knife. Poison dagger. He stabbed Frick in the leg. They took the knife. He put something in his mouth. They pinned him to the ground. They pried open his jaws. "Candy," he said. There was a capsule of fulminate of mercury. All he had to do was chew on the capsule and the whole room would blow up and everyone in it. They held his head back. They removed the capsule. They beat him unconscious.

Lights shift. She comes back to 1901.

Sasha has been in prison for ten years. Much of it in solitary confinement, in a dungeon. And Frick survived. And became a hero in the press, and the public turned against the workers and the strike was broken. It was said that we set back the American Labor Movement by 40 years.

Lights shift. She is 23.

I am in the visitor's room at the Western Pennsylvania Penitentiary. I am frightened. I haven't seen Sasha since he was arrested. I am waiting and then all of a sudden he's there. In a gray outfit. Looking thin. He has lost some hair. The guard is watching us. We have told the warden that I am E.G. Berkman, Sasha's sister. I am shaking in the knees. But I keep my hands steady so Sasha can't see. Ah Sasha. Hello, my love… He won't look at me. We sit together on the wooden bench. He steals small glances, but my eyes are too much for him… I don't know what to say. He murmurs "Emma, Emma, Emma…" I don't want to weep. At this moment I would gladly change places with him…

It is April and the sun is trying to creep through the barred windows of the visitor's room…

He has changed, shoulders hunched, spirit broken. Brown eyes full of despair.

A door slams somewhere in the hallway. Sasha jerks his head up. Our eyes meet. I am smiling. I don't know why. The guard comes to stand over us. "Your time's up." Sasha jumps to his feet. I feel so helpless. He kisses me, and I feel something pass from his mouth to mine. Then he is gone as quickly as he came.

Lights shift. 1901.

In my mouth was a message from Sasha. It said that I should go to Inspector Reed and try to get a second visit for the next day. But by the next day my identity had been discovered and no one was in the mood for doing Emma Goldman any favors. No, after that day I didn't see Sasha again for 9 years.

Lights shift.

Johann Most was a very jealous man. He fell in love with me, and he hated Sasha. When Sasha tried to kill Frick, Most turned against us. He publicly denounced Sasha-saying that Sasha's "dramatic heroics with a toy pistol" were ridiculous and that Sasha was doing the movement more good by being locked up on Murderer's Row than he could on the outside. Most was denying the very ideas he himself had put forth; just to make Sasha look like a villainous fool…I decided to challenge Most, and to compel him to explain his lies in public. I bought a horsewhip.

Lights shift. Music.

I am sitting in the front row of Most's lecture. My whip is under my coat. He gets up to face the audience. I get up too. "I came to demand proof of your insinuations against Alexander Berkman." There is instant silence. Then I hear him muttering something about "hysterical woman." I pull out my whip and leap at him. I get him across the face and then on the neck and shoulders, and then I break my whip across my knee and throw it at him. The crowd is outraged. "Beat her up! Throw her out!" I ran out of the hall.

Lights shift. Emma picks up the letters.

Oh Sasha, I know how long it took you to write each word, with freezing hands, how hard it was to come by pen and paper in solitary confinement...

She rips the letters slowly throughout the following:

Sometimes I wonder if my life has been worth living up to this point. Has anything been heard? Has the world shifted even a little? Here I am hiding, pretending to be a maid in someone's apartment, preparing to run off to Canada like some horse thief. I don't know... If you're buried under a ton of dirt, isn't it better to hack at it with the heel of your shoe, rather than turn away from the task for lack of a shovel? Isn't it better to fight for breath than to resign oneself to suffocation?

Anarchism is a process, not a finality.

Oh, Sasha, I am trying to be brave.

Lights shift. Emma stands. In the following section the bold text indicates a public speech.

Union Square 1893.

I am scheduled as the last speaker. I can hardly wait for my turn to come. When it finally does, I get up to speak and my knees are shaking. I step forward. I hear my name echoed from a thousand throats: "Emma! Emma! Emma" I begin: "Men and women..." Uproarious applause. The clapping seems to me to be like the wings of white birds fluttering.

Lights shift

Men and Women. It has often been suggested to me that the constitution of the United States is a sufficient safeguard for the freedom of its citizens. I have not been satisfied with such a

safeguard. The nations of the world, with centuries of international law behind them, have never hesitated to engage in mass destructions, while solemnly pledging to keep the peace. Those in authority always have, and still do, abuse their power and the instances when they do not do so are as rare as roses growing on icebergs.

Lights shift.

I remember one long-stemmed American Beauty Rose. A gift from Sasha before my first public speech. With this pen that had my name engraved and a note: "A token of my love and as a harbinger of luck on your first public quest."

Lights shift.

Remember Americans that those who fought and bled for your liberties were in their time considered as being against the law, as being dangerous disturbers and troublemakers. They not only preached violence, but they carried out their ideas by throwing tea into the Boston Harbor. They said, "Resistance to tyranny is obedience to God." They wrote a dangerous document, you may have heard of it, called the Declaration of Independence. A document that remains dangerous to this day.

Lights shift.

I remember the ship. It was called Elbe. We travelled in steerage. We were herded together like cows. Like cattle. I remember the sea. It terrified me; it was so beautiful. An expanse of blue, wide, restless... I felt freedom in each spray of salty water hitting my face. The last day I remember very well: Everybody was on deck. My sister Helena and I stood very close together. The Statue of Liberty emerged from the mist. There she was, a symbol of hope, opportunity. She held her torch high to light the way to the free country, the asylum for all oppressed peoples. Helena and I would find a place in the generous heart of America. Our spirits were high, our eyes filled with tears.

Lights shift.

We respect your patriotism. But may there not be different kinds of patriotism as there are different kinds of Liberty? I know many people, I am one of them, who were not born in this country—nor have they ever applied for citizenship—and yet they love America with deeper passion and greater intensity than many natives, whose patriotism is manifested by pulling, kicking and insulting those who do not stand up when the national anthem is played. Our patriotism is that of a man who loves a woman with open eyes. He is enchanted by her beauty, but he sees her faults. So we too, who know America, love her beauty and her richness, but with the same passionate emotion, we hate her superficiality, her cant, her corruption, her mad unscrupulous worship at the altar of The Golden Calf.

Lights shift.

Wild applause from Union Square. My first public speech is a success. Over time I get braver.

Lights shift.

Let us discuss homosexuality. The entire persecution and sentencing of Oscar Wilde is an act of cruel injustice on the part of the society, which condemned this man. Why is it still necessary in 1895 to deny and cover up a dominant sexual trait that has been a part of the greatest art in the world? Plato, Socrates, Sappho, Michelangelo, Wagner, Shakespeare—if his sonnets are an indication—and Oscar Wilde. Take the American Poet Walt Whitman, whose sex differentiation enriched his knowledge of and his

understanding for human complexities. Whitman's idea of universal comradeship was conditioned in his magnetic response to his own sex. So too is Oscar Wilde a beautiful soul whose poetry has enriched the world. His unjust persecution is proof that puritanism still reigns. You and I must now embark on a brave and courageous mission in the service of enlightenment and humanness, in opposition to this ignorance and hypocrisy.

Lights shift.

I had a lover in Paris. One night I went out on the town with some friends. We landed at the Rat Mort, a Montmartre cabaret at about two o'clock in the morning. We ordered champagne. Across from us sat a very pretty French prostitute. One of the men asked if he could invite her over to our table, and I said "Sure, why not?" So she came over and we laughed and danced. Then, some fellow raised his glass in a toast, "To E.G." I drank mine down in one gulp. Suddenly everything went black.

I wake up in a hotel room with a splitting headache and this French girl in my bed. "Rein du tout, Cherie; you felt a bit sick last night." "What happened to me? I feel like I've been poisoned. "Not quite, but one of the boys did pour a little cognac into your champagne. We had to carry you downstairs. We hailed a cab, but we couldn't make you get into it. You sat down on the pavement and shouted, 'I am Emma Goldman, the anarchist, and I will not be forced!' It took five of us to get you into a cab."

I can't remember a thing. How did you get in here? "I refused to let those men take you away without me. They could have been crooks intending to rob you." But you have lost all of your earnings for the night. Here is twenty francs for your trouble. "What do you mean by this insult? Do you think a girl who makes her living on the streets has no feelings? That she would turn away from a friend in distress? No. Nursing is not my profession and I will not be paid for it."

Eyes glowing with fury. Dark hair falling across one cheek. The morning light beautiful around her. I reach up and pull her down towards me and we...

I have fallen in love many times with all kinds of people...but I have only been married once. When I left Jacob, I said to myself "If I ever love a man again, I will give myself to him without being bound by the Rabbi or the law, and when that love dies, I will leave...without permission."

Lights shift.

Men and Women. The institution of marriage makes a parasite of woman. It incapacitates her for life's struggles, annihilates her social consciousness, paralyzes her imagination, and then imposes its gracious protection, which is in itself a snare. True emancipation begins neither at the polls nor in the courts. It begins in a woman's soul. Since woman's great misfortune has been that she was looked upon as either an angel or devil, her true salvation lies in being place on earth, namely in being considered human.

Lights shift.

My husband was impotent. But that had nothing to do with my objection to marriage as an institution. He was an immigrant like me, and I don't think he ever adjusted to the new country very well. Marrying Jacob was the one thing I ever did that pleased Abraham Goldman.

I saw my father a few weeks ago. Helena wrote to me that my father was on deaths' door. Instead of resting he had gone back to work at the factory. He had lost weight; down to 98 pounds. He was very weak. I go to my father's work and find him here shoveling cereal into small boxes on an assembly line. He looks up and sees me. He smiles.

He is the only Jew, a man of 79, still not familiar with the English language. Most of the workers around him are young men who enjoy playing pranks and tricks on the "sheeny" with the long beard and the dark eyes. I hear that they have repeatedly harassed and molested him, causing him to faint.

The sight of my father so ill softens my heart. I do not forgive his violence, but I no longer have energy to hate him. My childhood was not unique. I realize that. I have seen so many children born unwanted. Maimed by ignorance, and poverty. There are thousands and thousands of children in this country who need help. That is part of the reason I never became a mother. Also, I have a problem with an inverted womb. The doctors said I should have an operation. But I never had the time. I love children. But there's always the movement to think of…

Lights shift.

Men and Women! We are told that so long as the law makes the discussion of birth control a crime, birth control must not be discussed. In reply I wish to say that it is not the birth control movement, but the law, which will have to go. I stand as one of the sponsors of a worldwide birth control movement, a movement that aims to set women free from the terrible yoke and bondage of enforced pregnancy, a movement that demands the right of every child to be well born. I may be arrested, I may be thrown in jail, but I will never make peace with a system that degrades woman to a mere incubator, and which fattens her on innocent victims.

Lights shift.

After Paris I went to Vienna to study to become a midwife so I could help women in poverty give birth safely and receive abortions.

In Vienna four very important things happened to me: I heard a young man named Sigmund Freud give a lecture. I heard for the first time the music of Wagner. I saw Eleanora Duse on the stage...and I fell in love with Fredrich Nietzsche.

Lights shift.

Anarchism brings us to the consciousness of ourselves. Will it lead to revolution? Indeed it will. No real social change has ever come about without revolution. Anarchism is the theory of social harmony. It is the great surging, living truth that is reconstructing the world, and that will usher in the dawn.

Lights shift.

The first time I was arrested they grabbed me after a speech I gave at Union Square. There were three of them. They held my hands behind my back and pushed me against a wall. "Why am I being arrested?" I asked them. No response. "What am I being arrested for?!" "For being Emma Goldman," one of them replied...After that I got so used to being hauled away at a moment's notice by the authorities, that now I always carry a book with me when I go to a meeting. That was the worst thing about the first time; I was locked away without anything to read.

Lights shift.

Men and Women, I will remind you of two great Americans, undoubtedly unknown to you: Ralph Waldo Emerson and Henry David Thoreau. When Thoreau was placed in prison for refusing to pay his taxes, he was visited by Emerson, who said to him, "David, what are you doing in jail?" Thoreau replied, "Ralph, what are you doing outside, when honest people are in jail for their ideals?"

Lights shift.

Sasha carefully prepared his escape from the Western Pennsylvania Penitentiary. Several of our dear friends devoted all of their time to carrying out his directions.

They rented a house two hundred feet from the main gate of the prison. From the cellar of the house, a tunnel had to be dug underneath the prison wall and into the prison yard towards an outhouse, indicated by Sasha on his diagram. Sasha was to manage somehow to leave the cellblock, reach the outhouse unobserved, tear up its wooden flooring, and crawl through the tunnel into the cellar of the house where he would find citizen's clothes, money and cipher directions to meet our friends.

Because the sounds of digging might attract the attention of the lookouts on the prison wall, a woman was hired to play the piano and sing. At the first sign of danger she would stop her music as warning to the diggers underground. When she burst into song again they would resume their work. The comrades in the tunnel were met with terrible difficulties, trying to break through rock formations, nearly being asphyxiated by poisonous fumes, they decided to divert the tunnel's path to a new termination, an area in the middle of the prison yard a hundred feet from the cellblock door. I received a message through one of our comrades...

Sasha enters and watches Emma.

Sasha successfully escaped from the cellblock and had managed to make his way to the tunnel only to find a surprise. Just that morning, prison builders had emptied a wagonload of rocks right over the spot where the tunnel began. Sasha had to sneak back to the cellblock without being seen. Prison officials discovered the tunnel, but they were unable to find out for whom it was intended. They suspected Alexander Berkman, but they had absolutely no proof to support their charges. No clues were discovered, but they put Sasha in solitary confinement just in case.

Lights shift. Sasha enters and walks a small rectangle as Emma speaks:

There are two kinds of cells in most penitentiaries. One is a light hole, and the other a blind cell, or a dark hole. This is often referred to as the dungeon where a prisoner is kept in solitary confinement. It is a damp, dark room 52" by 107" with a small opening 7" long and 1 1/2" wide to let some air in. There is no bench, no window and no source of light. The prisoner receives two pieces of bread and two cups of water per day. I have been sent to the dungeon on several occasions for short periods, but Sasha has been kept in solitary confinement for months at a time.

Lights shift.

September 6, 1901. Three days ago.

I am in the visiting room of the Western Pennsylvania Penitentiary. The guard calls in prisoner 6742358. A skinny man comes towards me. He has lost all of his hair. The same gray suit. I look into his eyes. He looks away. We sit down on the bench.
Sasha and Emma both sit on the chair, she is facing out, he is facing away.
The guard stands beside us. We try to speak to each other. In Yiddish. The guard says, "Speak in English!" We try. It has been nine years. He won't look at me. The guard leans over us. "Your time's up!"

Lights shift.

I believe in Anarchy, Freedom,
Free love,
Speech.

I believe in America
Courage. People. Pride.
I believe
There is great work to do.
Now. However we can.
I believe
That governments abuse their power.
Now and always. I believe
The future is in our hands.
I believe in dreamers,
Children, streamers
Confetti. That
Dancing is important,
I believe
That if America has entered the war to make the world safe for Democracy, she must first make democracy safe in America.
I believe in peace.
Beauty.
Duty.
That people must be free to express themselves
Differently.
In Liberty.
I believe in passion. Art.
In anarchy.
That women must make choice about their lives, as wives. Mothers.
Lovers.
I believe that America should not stick her nose into other people's business.
I believe
Revolution coming next, in sex.
Tolstoy.
A brand new age.
Duse on stage.
I believe in Russia's cries,

In open eyes.
The president lies.
I believe in Anarchy.
In Freud's interpretations.
Humanity. Salvation.
I believe in action. Strikes.
The likes of which we've still not seen.
I believe in honesty.
Good food. Wine. Happiness. Radiance.
The free child. Oscar Wilde.
Sasha's smile.
Defiance. Pride. I believe
Anarchism is a process not a finality.
I believe in the spark,
A light in the dark.
History is nothing but eternal reoccurrence and people are still tearing
Each other apart
After all these years, while we fools go on …
Believing.
In life. Liberty.
The American people.
Awakening.
Emancipation. Liberation. Dreams. Ideals.
Anarchy.
I believe in standing alone, grown
Woman. Her
Face held high not afraid to die.
I am proud of my beliefs and
I believe, no matter what anyone says about me.
I believe in the masses.
In destroying the classes.
I believe in tenderness. In
Common sense. The declaration of
Independence.

I believe in Max, Johann, Fedya, Alexander Berkman. Ah Sasha...

I believe in free will and action.

I don't care what the newspapers say about me.

In resisting tyranny.

I believe in birth control.

Soul searching.

Reading. Writing. Watching.

Not so much to forgive, but to understand.

I believe in the brave heart,

A light in the dark... to continue

The fight, or wrong or for right...

I believe in Anarchy. And

Nietzsche says,

"That which is born out of love always takes place beyond Good and Evil"

Upheaval. Starting fresh.

Making a mess.

I believe in moving.

Not losing

Hope.

In coping with these hard but wonderful times.

Lines of people all over the world

Holding each other, helping each other.

Protesting war. Shouting for...

Freedom, free love, speech...

I believe in Anarchy...

"The philosophy of a new social order based on liberty, unrestricted by man-made law."

I believe in fun.

Running screaming, dancing laughing, leaping, kissing, wishing. Making it real.

I believe in Love.

Again and again.

Women and Men, and women

And all the men in my life.
I believe in living for today.
Strong. Resilient. Gay.
Paving the road.
I believe our enemy is the dying past and we are the
Glowing future.
I believe in we.
I believe in me.
You, her, him, them (as long as they're us) not to mention everybody who doesn't know yet.
I Believe
In charm. Strong arms.
The great alarm... Sasha still in prison, and
Here's to social harmony
And all the men in my life. I believe in going ahead.
The sharing of bread.
I believe in Anarchy. Freedom. Free love. Speech. I believe in America.
I disbelieve in authority, invasion, coercion and force. Oppression, violence, marriage, divorce.
I believe in the absence of government...
In people running their own lives.
Children not deprived.
Of love.
Free love. And the freedom
Of dreaming and making dreams live.
The pleasure to give
A warm hand
To the next man. Fortified
With courage and will.
Pulling each other up the hill.
I believe in anarchism.
The new world.
Women and men
Beginning again.

I believe in patriotism of the soul.
Our role
In the liberation of mankind.
I believe in the spiritual,
Political,
Economic,
Revolution of life. Strife.
I believe in doing whatever it takes
To make
It happen.
Lights shift.

I suppose I'll have that bath now. I'm not frightened. I've had a productive evening. I've torn up all the letters that were likely to involve my friends. I've thought of Sasha. And I've enjoyed all of this, the stories. It's so good to be able to look back to forgive oneself, to feel proud of the pain, and the silliness, and the lovemaking.

These are trying but wonderful times. There is great work to do. Be brave beloved comrades. Our enemy is fighting a losing battle. They are of the dying past. And we, we are of the glowing future.

> *The man's voice returns. During his speech, the lights slowly fade as Emma prepares for her bath. Towards the end of his speech, Emma gathers all the torn pieces of Sasha's letters, places them in the ashtray and sets them on fire as the lights slowly fade to black.*

MAN'S VOICE: At 10 o'clock on the night of September 9th, 1901, Emma Goldman was arrested for her alleged complicity in the plot to assassinate President McKinley. She was captured at the home of an anarchist friend, Max Baginsky. At the time of the discovery of her whereabouts, Emma Goldman was taking a bath. Twelve officers crowded into the apartment. The chief officer grabbed Emma Goldman's arm. "Who are you?" "I am the maid," she replied. When further questioned, the alleged maid claimed to be a Swedish servant girl who did not speak

English. The officers made a thorough search of the premises. One officer discovered a pen on the floor. The pen was engraved with the name Emma Goldman. The captain ordered three of his men to remain on the premises to await the return of the woman anarchist. Goldman realized the game was up. There was no way out. No sign of her friend returning home, no use keeping up her false identity. "Excuse me, officer," she said. All the policemen turned to look at her –

In fire light

EMMA: I am Emma Goldman.

> *Emma pours water over the flames.*
> *Blackout.*
> *End of Play*

The Snake And The Falcon

By Jessica Litwak

CHARACTERS: The characters are played by four or five actors. If the entire trilogy is produced Sasha can be played by a separate actor, if the play is done alone (or if the ensemble prefers) the role of Sasha can be incorporated into the roles of Actor Four. If this is done the lines designated by an asterisk * can be cut or given to Emma.

ACTOR ONE: Emma Goldman
ACTORE TWO: J. Edgar Hoover
ACTOR THREE: Female Reporter, Matron, Edith Wilson, Alice, Margaret Sanger, and Mrs. Hoover
ACTOR FOUR: Male Reporter, Mitchell Palmer, Ben Reitman, Don, Guard, Police Officer, Judge
ACTOR FIVE: Sasha (Alexander Berkman)

SETTING: The play takes place from 1917 to 1919. The set can easily transform into many places from The Missouri State Penitentiary to Ellis Island.
  / Indicates an overlap.

ACT ONE

Lights up on Emma Goldman's speaking platform in Union Square.

EMMA: THE GREAT WAR, The War of Nations,

The War to End all Wars?
In 1914 Wilson says, "America will be neutral."
But his promise is a futile dream
Because by 1917
The presidential candidate of peace
has taken out a lease
On War.

> *Lights up on J. Edgar Hoover's bedroom. As he dresses, he places a record on a Victrola: Italian Opera. His clothes are arranged alphabetically.*

J. EDGAR HOOVER: 1. Slippers off. Placed carefully in a box.
2. Robe off. Hung on a hanger. Next to shirt.
EMMA: The Machine gun, Ladies and Gentlemen,
Needs 6 men to fire it.
The shells tear flesh on impact.
And here's another fact about this war: Mustard gas.
The deadliest weapon in all this mess.
Deep in the trenches, it is colorless.
Blistering skin, vomiting, blind eyes,
Internal, external bleeding, then you die.
J. EDGAR HOOVER: 3. New socks from a drawer.
4. Shoes Carefully shined from a satin box.
EMMA: Ladies and Gentleman, I am pleading for the absence of war,
So the rich don't get richer on the bloodshed of the poor.
EDGAR: 5. Stiffly pressed white shirt from a hanger next to Tie.
EMMA: Mr. Man over there with his head down in the program!
Mrs. Woman concealing her blush with a paper fan!
Open your eyes and see,
That hiding your face is no way to be
Strong.
You think you are beyond the crush,
The rush

To political glory,
our National story
Is a tale of tears,
to see sweet boys of small years
Come back to us in box after box of hardened wood.
And should and should and should
We spend
Our hard earned cash making dead young men?

J. EDGAR HOOVER: 6. Tie Hung next to vest closer to pants.

EMMA: Hundreds of thousands of empty boots.
His mother saved his baby tooth.
He was just a kid from the lower east side.
Sent off too die
for a cause no one even explained to him.

J. EDGAR HOOVER: Tie on.

EMMA: Once more
Into the breach?
Just to hear the screech
of metal upon metal,
Just to win? To cheer?
As the flag of triumph waves?
Because America must own more slaves?
Be the powerful nation of kings,
Oh hear the sorrowed beating of her wings
The dove of peace flies high, she is gone,
Escaping another blood filled dawn.

J. EDGAR HOOVER: 7. Vest from hanger next to ties. Vest on. Buttoned.

EMMA: A little more death each day,
Don't wait around for those that pray,
To save you. Burn your draft card here
This war will not abolish fear
It will build it.
Into a fortress.

J. EDGAR HOOVER: 8. Shoes off. 9. Pants. Perfectly creased on a hanger next to Robe.
EMMA: Our soldier boys are tenement sons. The ones
From the working class under the grass long before their time.
The line stretches back to Ellis Island
where they landed, on boats from
Italy Ireland Russia China Africa France Greece
To the promise of the land of peace
And freedom.
And now they sail off again at morning light
to fight
For stripes and stars, to scar
The hemisphere with violent uselessness.
J. EDGAR HOOVER: 10. Pants on.
EMMA" This war, Ladies and Gentlemen
Is for fat cats in spats
Filling leather chairs, climbing the velvet stairs
Of enterprise.
Most of you adore the fight. It is the light
You live by.
But those of us, like Alexander Berkman and I,
who are riled up
by the Russian Revolution, see the persecution
Of the poor and disenfranchised as patriotism gone wrong.
But patriotism in America is valued higher than justice
and let me tell you Ladies and Gents
I'll be back in jail before the night is done.
J. EDGAR HOOVER: 11. Jacket from a hanger next to pants.
EMMA: Why it is lawful to yell "aim, fire!"
But against the law to moan "desire!"?
I believe in LOVE, ladies and gentlemen.
Wet lips and tongues, hands on skin. That is a win. That is how to save the world. With pearls.
Why is free Love a crime and expensive War a duty?

J. EDGAR HOOVER: 12. Belt on. 13. Shoes on.
14. Spats over shoes.
EMMA: The government asserts
Women cannot make love without giving birth.
So girls drink turpentine, roll downstairs, stick knitting needles and shoe-hooks into wombs
To free a seventh or ninth child from the doom
Of being born into hunger and poverty.
Like boys on the killing fields these girls yield
To death. But, ladies and gents what's the sense of losing lives when Charles Goodyear strived
To develop a vulcanized rubber. Flexible. Delicate. Strong.
THE CONDOM.
My friends. This is the weapon we need.
This is what American money should seed. Not into Mustard Gas. Not machine gun fire.
We require the instruments to make us free – not from each other but with each other, not against but for, not less but more. More love. More love. More love.
J. EDGAR HOOVER: 15. The hair combed neatly. 16. A touch of pomade.
EMMA: I believe in justice. For Black and White and sick and well
Homosexual and whore, the haves and the have nots, and the have mores.
The woman and man who stand
For freedom without guns. The equal ones.
I believe in a new America.
Where The Poor who are not cattle will refuse to fight the rich man's battle.

J. Edgar Hoover admires himself in the mirror

EMMA: Here is the telegraph wire: CEASE-FIRE,
Ladies and Gentleman.
Man over there with his head down in the program!

Woman over there concealing her blush with a paper fan!
You and You and You and You. It's time to do
The right thing and
Cry LOVE and Cry PEACE And Cry NOW.

> *Music off. A police officer jumps onto the stage. He grabs Emma and Sasha and drags them off. J. EDGAR HOOVER opens a briefcase. A knock at the door. He slams the case shut. Mrs. Hoover enters.*

J. EDGAR HOOVER: Mama!

> *She hands him a glass of milk.*

Mrs. HOOVER: Hard at work so late at night. And all dressed up. Do you have some midnight rendezvous?
J. EDGAR HOOVER: I'm very busy, Mama. You know I always dress to work. I think more clearly in a well-made suit.
Mrs. HOOVER: If you're in for the evening, my darling, come down and sit with your father.
J. EDGAR HOOVER: I sat with him this morning.
Mrs. HOOVER: He is asking for you.
J. EDGAR HOOVER: I start my new job tomorrow. I won't be any good to Papa if I fail to impress my new boss.
Mrs. HOOVER: Your new boss will find you indispensable, J'Edgar. You will know exactly what he wants before he knows himself.
J. EDGAR HOOVE: Then you'd better let me study up on him, Mama.
Mrs. HOOVER: Why are you so jumpy?
J. EDGAR HOOVER: I am not jumpy, Mama. Tomorrow is a big day-
Mrs. HOOVER: Don't worry about tomorrow, J'Edgar Boy. You are going to do great things with those government men. As long as you stay three steps ahead.
J. EDGAR HOOVER: Everything depends upon it, Mama. Now, please-

Mrs. HOOVER: Don't forget to drink your milk.

She exits. Lights shift. A courtroom. Emma and Sasha look at each other. Male Reporter enters, note pad in hand.

MALE REPORTER: The Espionage Act of 1917 prohibits all interference with military recruitment.

Female Reporter enters, note pad in hand.

FEMALE REPORTER: Based on their seditious anti-war propagandized public speeches,
MALE REPORTER: The U.S. Government now considers Emma Goldman and Alexander Berkman to be enemy spies.
FEMALE REPORTER: The criminals received the maximum sentence permitted by law: Two years in prison with a fine of 2,000 dollars apiece.
MALE REPORTER: Berkman is sentenced to the Tombs in New York City.
FEMALE REPORTER: Goldman to The Missouri State Penitentiary.

Lights shift.

SASHA: Prison again, Comrade.
EMMA: Prison again, Sasha.
SASHA: Be of good cheer. It is better to stay behind bars than to be MUZZLED in our freedom. Our spirits will not be daunted, nor our wills broken. Be brave, Comrade.
EMMA: Goodbye, Comrade.

Lights shift. Edgar's room. There is a knock at the window. Edgar opens it. Don climbs through.

J. EDGAR HOOVER: Did anybody see you?

DON: No. Your Mother made the front door impossible. So I climbed up the drainpipe like a cat burglar. But I was careful. As always. It's good to see you, Eddie.

He moves closer. Edgar steps back.

J. EDGAR HOOVER: From now on you have to call me Mr. Hoover.
DON: Mr. Hoover?
J. EDGAR HOOVER: Yes.

Don moves close to him.

DON: Have you missed me, Mr. Hoover?

J. Edgar Hoover reluctantly pushes him away.

J. EDGAR HOOVER: I called you here on government business.
DON: For The Justice Department?
J. EDGAR HOOVER: I will ask the questions tonight, Don!
DON: Some boys from Kappa Alpha Fraternity came by.
J. EDGAR HOOVER: What? When?
DON: They said they know things about you.
J. EDGAR HOOVER: What things?
DON: I don't want to repeat them.
J. EDGAR HOOVER: I am asking you to repeat them.
DON: I don't want you to get in a temper at me-
J. EDGAR HOOVER: DON!
DON: Things about your blood.
J. EDGAR HOOVER: My blood?
DON: They were saying something about you being just "white enough to pass".
J. EDGAR HOOVER: Those boys need to be handled with care, Don.
DON: They called me a faggot.
J. EDGAR HOOVER: Well that's just not true, is it Don?

DON: They threatened to beat me up if I didn't tell them where you live.

J. EDGAR HOOVER: What did you tell them, Don?

DON: I told them you don't work at the Library of Congress anymore. I told them I didn't know where to find you.

J. EDGAR HOOVER: And what if they try to find me?

DON: You've taught me well. I know how to hide things.

J. EDGAR HOOVER: What did you do?

DON: I switched the progression. Worked forwards. Found an unexpected anomaly. Went backwards. Switched again.

J. EDGAR HOOVER: Are you absolutely certain there is no trace?

DON: A birth record can be filed under child's name, city of birth, day of birth, health, year, street name, father, month, mother, or any anomaly to circumstance. I filed you so deep no one will ever find the details. You are safe.

J. EDGAR HOOVER: Thank you.

DON: You can trust me.

J. EDGAR HOOVER: I know.

J. Edgar Hoover kisses Don on the cheek.

J. EDGAR HOOVER: I need you tonight, Don.

Don gets down on his knees in front of J. Edgar Hoover.

J. EDGAR HOOVER: No.

J. Edgar Hoover pulls him back up to his feet.

J. EDGAR HOOVER: I need information. About my new boss. One day I will have a file on every single person that interests me, Don. I will own everyone's secrets. Right now I need Mitchell Palmer's.

DON: Radical anarchists tried to blow up his house.

J. EDGAR HOOVER: I can read about that in the papers.

DON: He's a close friend of President Wilson.
J. EDGAR HOOVER: Everyone has that.
DON: And even closer friend of Mrs. Wilson.
J. EDGAR HOOVER: Really?
DON: Yes.
J. EDGAR HOOVER: I need to find out what makes him tick.

Don takes a paper out of his jacket pocket and hands it to J. Edgar Hoover

J. EDGAR HOOVER: What's this?
DON: What makes him tick.

J. Edgar Hoover reads from the paper.

J. EDGAR HOOVER: "Communism is eating its way into our homes. The tongues of revolutionary heat are licking the alters of the churches, leaping into the belfry of the school bell, burning up the foundations of society."
DON: He's a fanatic about Reds.
J. EDGAR HOOVER: This is good, Don.
DON: I'm always looking out for you, Eddie. Mr. Hoover. I know what you want before you know yourself.
J. EDGAR HOOVER: You're a good boy, Don.
DON: I'm a lot older than you.
J. EDGAR HOOVER: You're still my boy though aren't you?
DON: I'm your boy.

Don touches his cheek.

DON: I get you information.

Don strokes down his arm.

DON: So you can move up in the world.

He undoes J. Edgar Hoover's belt.

DON: You have big ambition

He unzips J. Edgar Hoover's pants.

J. EDGAR HOOVER: You'll land me in prison, Don.

Don touches J. Edgar Hoover.

DON: I am too careful for that, Mr. Hoover.

J. Edgar Hoover groans with pleasure. Lights shift. Female Reporter enters.

FEMALE REPORTER: 1918

Male Reporter enters.

MALE REPORTER: November 11, 1918 to be precise.
FEMALE REPORTER: Thanks to The Paris Peace Conference
MALE REPORTER: The Treaty of Versailles to be exact.
MALE AND FEMALE REPORTER: ARMISTICE!

Lights shift. Prison.

EMMA: ARMISTICE! ARMISTICE!

Matron enters.

MATRON: What you yelling about, Goldman?
EMMA: The war is over! The troops are headed home! The Guards were shouting about it.
MATRON: Calm down, Goldman. A woman of your age getting all worked up. It's indecent.

EMMA: Will the political prisoners be released? Will Alexander Berkman and I be free?

MATRON: Don't get excited. We're keeping all the foreigners locked up tight. Especially the Reds.

EMMA: I'm an American.

MATRON: You are an immigrant!

Lights shift. Male Reporter enters

MALE REPORTER: Immigration.

Female Reporter enters.

FEMALE REPORTER: 1789:

MALE REPORTER: The United States Constitution:

FEMALE REPORTER: Any Alien. Being a free white person, may be admitted to become a citizen.

MALE REPORTER: As long as he makes forced renunciation of allegiance to any other country.

FEMALE REPORTER: 1882: The Chinese Exclusion Act keeps America from being overrun by Asians.

MALE REPORTER: 1906: All immigrants now required to learn English.

FEMALE REPORTER: 1907: Any woman with US citizenship forfeits it if she marries a foreigner.

MALE REPORTER: The Immigration Act of 1917 bars entry of / anarchists-

FEMALE REPORTER: "Anarchists", "polygamists", "idiots," "feeble-minded persons," "epileptics," "insane persons, "alcoholics", "professional beggars," all persons "mentally or physically defective"

MALE REPORTER: 1919

FEMALE REPORTER: America is / blessed

MALE REPORTER: Cursed, by a surge of

FEMALE REPORTER AND MALE REPORTER: IMMIGRATION

MALE REPORTER: Men, women and children
FEMALE REPORTER: Flooding through Ellis Island into
FEMALE REPORTER AND MALE REPORTER: New York.

Male and Female Reporter speak simultaneously

FEMALE REPORTER: Dirty Russians, Dirty Irish, Polish, Italian, African, Catholic, Jewish, Dirty Greeks, Chinese, Muslims, Indians. Oh and, those Dutch.
MALE REPORTER: A mosaic of incongruous discordant harmonious varied cultures. A new kind of city made up of a million pieces of different colored glass.
FEMALE REPORTER: A great green statue
MALE REPORTER: Stands in the harbor.
FEMALE REPORTER: "At our sea-washed,
MALE REPORTER: Sunset gates
FEMALE REPORTER: Shall stand a mighty woman with a torch,
MALE REPORTER: Whose flame is the imprisoned lightning,
FEMALE REPORTER: And her name:
MALE REPORTER and FEMALE REPORTER: Mother Of Exiles."
FEMALE REPORTER: President Woodrow Wilson warns the nation
MALE REPORTER: "The Hyphenated Americans have poured the poison of disloyalty into the very arteries of our national life."
FEMALE REPORTER: In America, a new threat is born.
MALE REPORTER: A terror the color of blood.
FEMALE REPORTER and MALE REPORTER: RED SCARE.

Lights out on Reporters. Lights up on J. Edgar Hoover pacing outside of Mitchell Palmer's office. Palmer enters. J. Edgar Hoover jumps up and offers his hand.

J. EDGAR HOOVER: Excuse me? Sir? It's Hoover, Sir. John Edgar Hoover. I have waited nearly five days to meet you, Sir.
PALMER: Aren't you the hustling young fellow who works all night and never goes home?

J. EDGAR HOOVER: I go home, Sir.
PALMER: But you prefer it here.
J. EDGAR HOOVER: Yes Sir.
PALMER: They call you Speed for all the case forms you pile up so fast.
J. EDGAR HOOVER: I'm a hard worker, Mr. Palmer.
PALMER: Don't you have a girl somewhere who wants your attention of an evening?
J. EDGAR HOOVER: I live with my parents, Sir.
PALMER: How old are you?
J. EDGAR HOOVER: 24.
PALMER: Don't your folks want you out of their house?
J. EDGAR HOOVER: I am their sole provider, Sir.
PALMER: What's wrong with your father, can't he work?
J. EDGAR HOOVER: I'd prefer not to discuss my father, Sir.
PALMER: If you work for me we'll discuss any damn thing I want to discuss. Wait a minute. If I'm not mistaken, there was something fuzzy in your background.
J. EDGAR HOOVER: Fuzzy, Sir?
PALMER: Unanswered questions, if I recall. There does not appear to be any official record of your birth.
J. EDGAR HOOVER: I will look into that, Sir.
PALMER: What about the war, Hoover.
J. EDGAR HOOVER: All for it, Sir.
PALMER: I'm a Quaker.
J. EDGAR HOOVER: Yes, Sir.
PALMER: Otherwise I would have served. I was not afraid to fight.
J. EDGAR HOOVER: No, Sir. They call you The Fighting Quaker.
PALMER: Woodrow Wilson and I worked side by side to send America to war when we deemed it necessary. We raided the country for draft dodgers. What about you Hoover?
J. EDGAR HOOVER: I had to take care of my family, Sir.
PALMER: That family again.
J. EDGAR HOOVER: I have constantly sought out new responsibilities, Sir.

PALMER: We've established that you're ambitious Hoover. But Washington is teeming with smart boys. Good looking ones too. You aren't the only sharp dresser in town.

J. EDGAR HOOVER: I worked my way through college as a clerk at The Library of Congress, Sir.

PALMER: So?

J. EDGAR HOOVER: I mastered the Library of Congress filing system and then mastered the Dewey Decimal system. The system divides all knowledge into twenty-one basic classes, each identified by a single letter of the alphabet. Most of these alphabetical classes are further divided into more specific subclasses, identified by two-letter, or occasionally three-letter, combinations. Each subclass includes a loosely hierarchical arrangement of the topics pertinent to the / subclass-

PALMER: I have a full day, Hoover.

J. EDGAR HOOVER: You see, Sir, I mastered it so well they doubled my salary. It was as if I found a new language. It spoke to me and I spoke to it. I stayed up for nights on end in that Library with that system. You might say I discovered its true purpose.

PALMER: Which is what, Hoover?

J. EDGAR HOOVER: I can use it to locate any single item I want. Including people. It is in my power to track any person in this country of 105 million souls.

And that's not all, Sir. I can use it to hide things. Just by manipulating the code.

PALMER: Manipulating the code?

J. EDGAR HOOVER: I have a dream, Sir, that one day there will be an entire agency of investigation that will be able to find things that have been hidden and hide things that should never be found.

PALMER: I don't like private detectives.

J. EDGAR HOOVER: No Sir. Not Private. Federal. A Federal Agency of Investigation. And we will have a file on everyone suspected of anything from betrayal to sabotage. With these files, we'd be able to track terrorists. Sir, on June 2nd a band of radical anarchists sent 30 mail bombs to government officials. Only a few reached their targets. One exploded outside your home, Sir. You, who could be the next President of the United States.

PALMER: You know what those letter bombs are Hoover?

J. EDGAR HOOVER: Treason, Sir.

PALMER: They are treason. But those reds have it wrong. These attacks will only increase our force. This country is being destroyed by immigration! 256,000 Russians in one year alone. 289,000 Italians. Up to 12,000 aliens a day streaming in from Ellis Island.

J. EDGAR HOOVER: Yes, Sir.

PALMER: And you know where the epicenter of that alien revolution is Hoover?

J. EDGAR HOOVER: Moscow?

PALMER: New York City!

J. EDGAR HOOVER: A terrible place, Sir.

PALMER: And up in Albany, you got working class immigrant mick Al Smith running the state, opening the gates for more and more rats. And you know what the immigrants are spawning Hoover?

J. EDGAR HOOVER: A vigorous propaganda in favor of Bolshevism, Sir?

PALMER: Bolshevik Propaganda! And you know who is leading the ruin of America?

J. EDGAR HOOVER: The Jews?

PALMER: The Jews. It's a Jewish led conspiracy. Know how I know that Hoover? The War department Military Intelligence Division On Jews. Bet you didn't even know there was such an office.

J. EDGAR HOOVER: Actually, Sir, I /did

PALMER: Do you know how we're going to get them, Hoover?

J. EDGAR HOOVER: Probable cause.

PALMER: Good Boy. Preventative Detention. If we think they might break a law, we drag them in. Clear the streets.

J. EDGAR HOOVER: And then what, Sir?

PALMER: Fill the prisons with them!

J. EDGAR HOOVER: I disagree!

PALMER: WHAT? YOU WHAT?

J. EDGAR HOOVER: We have got to get them out, Mr. Palmer. Out of the country. Off our soil. Ship them back to the countries they came from. I have an idea, Sir! We could use Ellis Island as a deportation portal – the very place that welcomed them in can give them the heave-ho.

PALMER: Goodness Hoover, what an idea!

J. EDGAR HOOVER: We can round them up in massive raids. Like your draft dodgers.

PALMER: We need a high profile case. Something that tells the country we mean business. We need to get rid of someone big.

J. EDGAR HOOVER: We need to do it now, Sir. Communism is forcing its way into our homes, our churches, our schools, and the foundations of our society. I am like a snake, Mr. Palmer. I can slither unseen and strike when least expected. I can make you famous.

PALMER: I am famous.

J. EDGAR HOOVER: Of course, Sir. I mean I can put you in the history books.

PALMER: We'll take it to the President!

J. EDGAR HOOVER: The President? No one has been allowed to see President Wilson since his accident.

PALMER: He'll see me.

J. EDGAR HOOVER: He will?

PALMER: I'll go in through the wife. First Lady has a bit of crush.

J. EDGAR HOOVER: That is not surprising, Sir.

PALMER: Can you do this Hoover? Come up with a case big enough to knock the socks off America?

J. EDGAR HOOVER: I can do this, Sir.

PALMER: You do it and I'll put you in charge of a whole new division of the Justice Department. A Spy Agency or whatever. How does that sound?

J. EDGAR HOOVER: That sounds, well, beautiful, Sir. It sounds just beautiful.

PALMER: You go fishing, Hoover, catch me one great big communist fish, and we'll send him back to the seas from whence he came. Then the doors of deportation will swing wide.

J. EDGAR HOOVER: Yes, Sir!

PALMER: But we are going to have to grow you up, Hoover.

J. EDGAR HOOVER: Grow me up, Sir?

PALMER: Get you a wife. And a home of your own.

J. EDGAR HOOVER: A wife?

PALMER: Yes. I'll send someone over this afternoon.

Lights shift. Emma in her prison cell. Matron enters. Matron throws some wilted flowers at Emma.

MATRON: These came for you.

EMMA: They are almost dead.

MATRON: Do I look like a florist? GET UP GOLDMAN, you are late for the shop!

EMMA: I don't feel well. I thought the doctor would give me the day off, it being my birthday.

MATRON: Yeah. Maybe you'll get a cake and a clown.

EMMA: You didn't deliver my gifts. Margaret said she was sending oranges. Ben sent homemade preserves. There was a card-

MATRON: Get up!

EMMA: I heard there were 50 signers of a birthday greeting, but I haven't seen it-

MATRON: Shut your mouth and stand the hell up.

EMMA: I am 50 years today, Matron. Hips hurt. Hands swollen.

MATRON: I don't need to listen to your sob story, Goldman. You were supposed to be at your sewing machine fifteen minutes ago.

EMMA: 50 years, Matron. 30 of them on the firing line.

MATRON: The foreman is gonna send you to the hole if you don't start pressing your peddle. What are you doing?

Emma writes.

EMMA: I am writing something very important, Matron. If you are a good girl, I'll read it to you.
MATRON: Another Bolshevik speech?
EMMA: A report on prison conditions.
MATRON: Let me see that!
EMMA: It's not finished.
MATRON: Who you writing a report for, Goldman? Commie headquarters?

Matron grabs the paper out of Emma's hands.

EMMA: The Governor of Missouri will be ashamed to see how women are treated in his prisons.

Matron shoves it back at Emma.

MATRON: LET ME HEAR IT!
EMMA: You sure you don't want me to teach you how to read?
MATRON: Shut up!

Emma reads.

EMMA: "The Missouri State Penitentiary is run on the Merit system. To attain the letter A, means to have your sentence reduced, or to receive special favors, like an extra visiting hour or a small piece of fruit."
MATRON: Sounds fair to me for a bunch of murderers, thieves and treasonous crooks.
EMMA: "But if we don't meet our quota of 120 jackets a day, we have no chance of any merit whatsoever. In fact we are brutally punished. There is no regard for age or physical limitations. The shop foreman is a brutal man. There is frequent flogging, deprivation, and solitary confinement in a blind cell, called The Hole where we are strung up by the wrists."

MATRON: You ain't seriously thinking I'm gonna let you write this, Goldman.

The Matron grabs the paper rips it to shreds. Emma tries to get the paper away from her; the Matron kicks Emma, who falls hard on the floor of the cell.

EMMA: Never rip a person's words! Destroying someone's writing is like destroying her soul.

MATRON: You want me to call the guard? Put you in the hole?

EMMA: Where is Minnie?

MATRON: You are just tryin' to get out of your task. You can't sew worth a doo doo and your always fallin' behind. Your hands are clumsier than a retard on whiskey. It's almost funny watching you try to get a jacket done. Fingers akimbo.

EMMA: They bleed.

MATRON: Whine. Whine. Whine. All the time whinin' to the girls who never said nothin' 'bout the task 'til you brought your fat mouth in here. You are up to mischief, Goldman. You lucky you ain't in the men's side.

EMMA: The male prisoners at least have books to read. The women have none! The food on our side is rancid and cold.

Matron slaps her.

EMMA: Where is Minnie?

MATRON: You ain't the boss in here! Bad things happen to people who make trouble. Might do you well to be a little more afraid. Now get up!

EMMA: My young comrade Minnie was like a ray of sunshine when she got here. No one could believe such a fragile slip of a girl could be serving 22 years. The inmates always asked her: What are you in for, Honey? Soliciting men? No. Picking pockets? No. Well what then? She smiled sweetly. For being an anarchist, she said.

MATRON: STOP SPEECHIFYING, GOLDMAN!

EMMA: Minnie was too weak to make her allotted task and she used pennies sent from her sister in Chicago to pay other inmates for help. But one-day dizziness overcame her.

MATRON: This ain't none of your business.

EMMA: She fainted and vomited. You force fed her and threw water on her and dragged her back to her machine.

MATRON: YOU ALL MUST MAKE THE TASK, NO SUCH THING AS I CAN'T!

EMMA: You beat her!

MATRON: I PUNISH CHEERFULLY, MARK YOU THAT.

EMMA: I heard Minnie's moans growing fainter every day.

MATRON: SHE'S A BOLSHEVIK TERRORIST, SAME AS YOU. AN ANIMAL.

EMMA: NOW I CAN'T HEAR HER AT ALL.

She slaps Emma again.

EMMA: If you want me to go to the shop you'll have to carry me yourself.

MATRON: I can't lift you myself. You're too fat. Tell you what, Goldman, you be a good girl and get up and I'll give you your letters.

EMMA: Letters?

MATRON: Three of 'em. Came this morning. Birthday letters. Got 'em right here. Go to the shop on your own steam and you'll get your letters at suppertime.

EMMA: I'll go to the shop on my own steam. But I want my letters first. If you don't give me my letters now, you're going to have to drag me.

MATRON: Last time I tried to move you I threw my damn back out.

EMMA: Yeah.

Matron takes three letters out of her pocket and throws them on the ground. Emma grabs them.

MATRON: Birthday cards from Bolshevik sex fiends?
EMMA: Sasha. Ben. Margaret Sanger.
MATRON: That Birth Control Witch? She wrote to you? She's famous.
EMMA: I am more famous than she is.
MATRON: My Preacher talked on Mrs. Sanger last Sunday. Read that one to me!
EMMA: These are private.
MATRON: You think prisoners are the only ones who get bored in here? Go on, it'll buy you a few more minutes off the machine!
EMMA: No.
MATRON: I could just tear 'em up. Destroy someone's soul-

Emma opens the first one and reads silently.

MATRON: Out loud, Goldman!
EMMA: She says she isn't coming to see me. She's too busy. She won't make the time to visit, even though she's traveling through Missouri on a speaking tour.
MATRON: Not so high and mighty are you, Goldman?
EMMA: I discovered her.
MATRON: Yeah. Sure you did.
EMMA: She approached me after a rally at Union Square; she said my voice was like a thunder through the crowds.
MATRON: You are loud alright, like a milk cow in labor.
EMMA" She hadn't done any public speaking, so I let her share the platform with me at a factory strike and then at a birth strike rally. She loved the subject of voluntary motherhood.
MATRON: How come you never had children, Goldman?
EMMA: Margaret's mother had birthed eleven children and it nearly killed her.
MATRON: You don't believe in having babies?
EMMA: Margaret said: "For the poor the menace of pregnancy hangs like a sword over women's heads."

MATRON: You are so busy messing up America you ain't even a human woman no more. Did you use birth control too?
EMMA: Of course.
MATRON: That is just pathetic and sad. What kinda woman don't want babies?
EMMA: Many women don't want babies, Matron. It so happens I am not one of them. I wanted children very badly. I couldn't have them.
MATRON: Read another one.
EMMA: I have counted on her visit. Visitors bring information and sustenance. They give us a purpose for living. I so miss having an intellectual companionship with a kindred spirit.
MATRON: Blah, blah, blah. Read that one there!

Emma opens another letter.

EMMA: Sasha.
MATRON: Who is Sasha? Your girlfriend?
EMMA: Sasha is Alexander Berkman.
MATRON: Boyfriend?
EMMA: Sasha is my spiritual and political partner.
Lights up on Sasha in a prison cell scribbling on a small scrap of paper.
SASHA: Happy Birthday, Beloved Emma. I hope they are giving you a party at the penitentiary. I bribed a guard for this pencil with money that Mollie sent. I've been locked in the hole for protesting about the unprovoked beating to death of a black inmate. My breathing is bad and the leg... but I've got nothing to complain about compared to others. I have bad news Emma – I don't want to write it in your birthday card, but I don't know when I will again have the chance of a pencil and the hopes of letter transport. Our friend D has killed himself in his cell. He left a note it said "Farewell Comrades. Struggle without fear, fight bravely."

Lights out on Sasha.

MATRON: You gonna kill yourself? Not on my watch. I ain't cutting you down if you string yourself up from a pipe. That will throw my back out for sure. Read the third one.
EMMA: I can't.
MATRON: Why the hell not?
EMMA: It's from Ben.
MATRON: Who is Ben?
EMMA: My lover. Or he was. His letters are like swallowing hot coals. He is married now and is expecting a child. Last time he wrote to me he spoke only about little nightgowns awaiting the baby. Even a birthday letter will hurt too much to bear.
MATRON: READ IT! OR I WON'T GIVE YOU THE ORANGES!

Emma opens Ben's letter. Lights up on Ben.

BEN: Dear Little Mommy, Is it your Birthday again? Wasn't it your birthday when we were in the Bellingham jail and then four years ago with me in Queens County and you on trial in New York, then me in Warrenville Prison and now you in Jefferson City? On this birthday I am in New York, the city where you worked and struggled. It is sad to imagine my little bright-eyed Mommy in prison garb with the pain of forced labor written on her face.
EMMA: Minnie died on the floor of her cell, Ben. They killed her. It's terrible here.
MATRON: STOP THAT!
BEN: We all send you love and hope that the coming year sets you free.

Emma closes the letter. Lights out on Ben.

EMMA: Where is Minnie?

MATRON: GET UP.

EMMA: The conditions here are outrageous. Before I am done I will avenge Minnie and change things in here. We will have hot food and books and outdoor excursions. A picnic! We will have a picnic!

MATRON: A picnic?

EMMA: With baskets of chicken.

MATRON

You ain't getting no one to let you on a picnic.

EMMA: Watch me.

The Matron shifts from foot to foot.

MATRON: I don't like you, Goldman. You pull at my brain and make me feel shifty. I just don't know anymore.

EMMA: What don't you know?

MATRON: I don't know if I want to kiss you or kick you.

EMMA: Just bring me my oranges.

She kicks Emma. Emma wails in pain.

MATRON: Happy Birthday.

Lights Shift. Palmer enters J. EDGAR HOOVER's office

PALMER: Where's my Fish?

J. EDGAR HOOVER: I am getting close, Sir. You'll have his name on your desk by end of day.

PALMER: That is your promise?

J. EDGAR HOOVER: That is my solemn promise.

PALMER: Then press your best suit and shine your best shoes. Edith Wilson has sent me an invitation. We're headed to the White House in three days.

J. EDGAR HOOVER: You're kidding, Sir.

PALMER: Kidding is not in my nature Hoover. How is the girl working out?

J. EDGAR HOOVER: The girl, Sir?

PALMER: Alice. The girl I sent over. One of my best. I gave her to you as an incentive gift.

J. EDGAR HOOVER: She's an excellent typist Sir.
PALMER: Her typing is not the reason I sent her to you.
J. EDGAR HOOVER: No Sir. You are trying to grow me up.
PALMER: For one of the Bright Young Men you are a tad dim in certain areas. Here she comes.

Alice enters.

PALMER: Alice.
ALICE: Good day, Mr. Palmer, Sir. Good Day Mr. Hoover.
PALMER: Remember your instructions, Hoover.
J. EDGAR HOOVER: Yes Sir.

Palmer exits.

J. EDGAR HOOVER: I need my fish today Alice! Have you found anyone at all?
ALICE: I did find this one thing, Sir.
J. EDGAR HOOVER: What did you find Alice?
ALICE: It might be too small a detail.
J. EDGAR HOOVER: There is no such things as too small a detail.
ALICE: This one prisoner in Missouri. An Anarchist. I copied a speech she did at a recent gathering. I'm not sure if she's your fish, I mean she's fifty years old, but she gives out birth control and was against the war-
J. EDGAR HOOVER: Some old woman can't be my big fish.
ALICE: I know she's just a woman, Sir, but I was hoping this might help you at least in some small way. Her file, Sir.

She hands him a file.

J. EDGAR HOOVER: I like you very much, Alice. You are a hard worker and a trustworthy friend. You are loyal and punctual, and your handwriting is very precise. I would like you to marry me.
ALICE: Excuse me, Sir?

J. EDGAR HOOVER: You are being promoted. Ha-ha.

ALICE: Promoted, Sir?

J. EDGAR HOOVER: To the role of wife. I have just promoted you to Wife.

ALICE: Are you proposing marriage, Mr. Hoover?

J. EDGAR HOOVER: I am, Alice. I am.

ALICE: But you don't even know me.

J. EDGAR HOOVER: You have a nice face. A good family. Don't think I didn't check. You come from good stock and are remarkably bland. Which is a very good thing, in my book, a very good thing. Some men like a little wildness. A tiny anarchy as it were. I am a solid Red-blooded American boy. I don't drink. I love baseball. Respect my mother. Nothing complicated. Nothing unsure. What do you say Alice?

ALICE: I'm in shock Sir.

J. EDGAR HOOVER: I am moving up in the world. Mitchell Palmer is sending me to New York. I am going to be heading up the raids against alien insurgents. Me. The head of my own division at 24 years old! You'll be sitting pretty. The wife of a famous man. Well Alice, what do you think?

ALICE: I don't really know you, Sir.

J. EDGAR HOOVER: OK. OK. Righto. Only fair. In order to gain your trust I need to trade something. I've done research on you. You should get something on me. A confession. How does that sound?

ALICE: Well, I don't really need-

J. EDGAR HOOVER: Nonsense. You deserve it. OK. This isn't easy, Alice. I'll need you to sign a letter of confidentiality.

ALICE: A letter, Sir?

J. EDGAR HOOVER: No, you're right. OK. Palmer would slap me. One can't build a life of trust without taking a risk. Sit down, Alice. Here goes. My father is mentally ill. He had to leave his position and can no longer work. I've had to care for him for years now. On my own steam. He's a good man but sometimes I don't think he even knows me. He looks blankly as if he's looking right through me. Oh My. This is private, Alice. You are the only human being outside my family with whom I have spoken about this.

ALICE: I am so sorry about your Father, Mr. Hoover.

J. EDGAR HOOVER: Call me Edgar. We're going to be husband and wife.

ALICE: I can't marry you, Sir.

J. EDGAR HOOVER: Oh. You're worried about genetics. I see. But calm yourself, Alice. Obviously my Father's malady is not hereditary. Look at me; I am sharp as a tack. So there is no need to distress about our children.

ALICE: It's not that.

J. EDGAR HOOVER: What is it then?

ALICE: I am already engaged.

J. EDGAR HOOVER: WHAT?

ALICE: I am so sorry, Sir. I should have said.

J. EDGAR HOOVER: You certainly "should have said"! This is terribly disappointing Alice. Terribly. Especially in the light of my recent disclosure. Can't you break it off?

ALICE: He just got back from the war, Mr. Hoover. That would be cruel.

J. EDGAR HOOVER: He'll get over it. He'll find another girl. Girls love soldiers. Does he have both his legs?

ALICE: Mr. Hoover. Can I ask you something?

J. EDGAR HOOVER: What is it?

ALICE: Why do you want to marry me?

J. EDGAR HOOVER: I am a rising star. I need a wife.

ALICE: I see.

J. EDGAR HOOVER: So what do you say, Alice?

ALICE: The thing is, I love this boy. The soldier.

J. EDGAR HOOVER: You'll get over him. It's sympathy. You're a kind-hearted girl. My mother said so. My mother approved of you a great deal.

ALICE: I admire you, Sir. I really do. I see what you are doing for America, but I just cannot marry you.

J. EDGAR HOOVER: No?
ALICE: No.
J. EDGAR HOOVER: That's your final answer?
ALICE: Yes sir.
J. EDGAR HOOVER: Alice?
ALICE: Yes, Mr. Hoover?
J. EDGAR HOOVER: You're fired.

Alice exits. Hoover is alone. Then he opens Alice's file. He reads:

J. EDGAR HOOVER: "I believe in Anarchy. Freedom-

As he reads lights come up on the opposite side of the stage. Emma speaks with him. As the speech goes on J. EDGAR HOOVER slowly stands.

EMMA and J. EDGAR HOOVER
…Free love, speech. I believe in America. Courage people pride that there is great work to do now however we can. I believe that governments abuse their power now and always

J. EDGAR HOOVER stops reading and listens as EMMA continues:

EMMA: I believe that if America has entered the war to make the world safe for democracy, she must first make democracy safe in America. I believe in Russia's cries, in open eyes. The President lies.
J. EDGAR HOOVER: MY FISH!

Lights out on Emma. Hoover skims the rest of the file.

J. EDGAR HOOVER: Kovno, Lithuania. Where the hell is that? Ellis Island at the age of 16. Ellis Island, perfect. You're a whore, Goldman. And your goose is cooked!

A picnic on the prison ground. Matron is watching Emma. An armed guard is pointing a gun at Emma's face as she tries to eat.

EMMA: This isn't exactly what I imagined.
MATRON: It's a picnic. You got your chicken.
EMMA: How do you know it's chicken?
MATRON: What else could it be?
EMMA: Fried anarchist.
MATRON: Save the comedy. You have 15 minutes out here. You should be grateful you got this far.
EMMA: I am happy for the reforms, don't get me wrong. It's the first warm meal old Addie over there has had in ten years.
MATRON: Why do you fret so over that Colored who killed her own husband?
EMMA: In self-defense. He was raping her. I've secured a job for her in Chicago when she gets out.
MATRON: She'll never get out.
EMMA: I have friends who are helping me fight her appeal; they think she'll be out be end of the year.
MATRON: Even if it works, I heard the Warden scaring her off. He told her, 'Goldman's friends are dangerous Bolshevik spies. They'll make you have sex and rob banks.' Scared the poor Colored half to death. Shaking in her boots. If she had boots. You are not eating.
EMMA: My appetite is somewhat stymied by the rifle.
MATRON: Guard lower the rifle.
GUARD: She's dangerous, Missus.
MATRON: I can subdue her if need be.

He lowers the gun.

EMMA: I want a picnic every two weeks without guards with guns in our faces, so that every two weeks the women will be given the chance to eliminate the prison from their consciousness. That sense of freedom and release will create a new morale

that will increase production in the shop and peace in the corridors.
MATRON: Guard.

He raises the gun.

EMMA: You have beautiful hair, Matron.

Emma stands takes a chuck of Matron's hair in one hand kisses it.

GUARD: That's enough of that.

Emma grins. Lights shift.
The White House. J. Edgar Hoover paces nervously.
Palmer enters.

J. EDGAR HOOVER: Mr. Palmer.
PALMER: Are you ready?
J. EDGAR HOOVER: I must confess to butterflies in the stomach, Sir.
PALMER: That is natural the first time. But play your cards right and you'll be in the White House under more Presidents than Woodrow Wilson.
J. EDGAR HOOVER: Yes, Sir.
PALMER: But remember for today she's the top man and we treat her as such until we get control of the situation. You've got the fish?
J. EDGAR HOOVER: I have the fish.
PALMER: Who is he?

Edith Wilson enters.

EDITH: Mitchell Palmer.
PALMER: Ma'am.
EDITH: And this must be the young fellow I spoke to you about. J. Edgar Hoover.

J. EDGAR HOOVER: It is an honor to meet you Ma'am.

EDITH: Mr. Hoover can wait in the outer office while we speak.

PALMER: I'd like him with us, Ma'am.

EDITH: These are highly sensitive matters of state.

PALMER: I can vouchsafe his confidence. How is the President?

EDITH: We have been concerned for your family after the bomb, Mitchell. I understand your house repairs are finally complete and your wife has regained her equilibrium.

PALMER: Yes. Thank you, Ma'am. How is the President?

EDITH: I heard you made a comment to a reporter.

PALMER: Pardon me?

EDITH: You told a newspaperman in New York that he probably knew more than the entire cabinet about the state of the President's health.

PALMER: You know the press, Ma'am.

EDITH: I know the press very well, Mitchell.

J. EDGAR HOOVER: Excuse me, Ma'am, but...

PALMER: Hoover...

J. EDGAR HOOVER: ...Mr. Palmer was just deflecting the onslaught of gossipmongers to protect The President.

EDITH: It sounded like a gripe.

PALMER: No Ma'am. Of course I've wanted to see the President. Hear his voice. We've been worried. We've wanted to know. The entire country wants to know.

EDITH: Many people have criticized the fact that I've kept him hidden in his bedroom. But the solitude is necessary. The doctor agrees.

PALMER: I'm sure you and the doctor are doing what is best.

EDITH: I know they are saying that the decisions coming out of the White House are being made by a woman.

PALMER: And how exactly are decisions being made, Ma'am?

EDITH: By the doctor and myself, Mr. Palmer.

PALMER: Political decisions, Ma'am?

EDITH: Medical decisions. But I'm no fool, Mitchell. I've watched the President for many long years. Do you think I am some nincompoop from the secretarial pool?

PALMER: Of course not.

EDITH: You are a good soldier, Palmer. My husband has always believed you are a straightforward man.

PALMER: Straightforward as they come, ma'am.

EDITH: I am not so sure about that, Palmer. Not so sure as my husband. I think you are driven by ambition and a hunger for revenge. I am not sure if that is good or bad, but I think whatever drives you isn't very Quaker.

PALMER: Ma'am-

EDITH: The Vice President wants to assume the President's powers. High-ranking advisors believe that this is the appropriate action given my husband's current inability to attend public functions. What is your opinion, Mitchell?

PALMER: I don't know…

EDITH: Please. Be frank. It's why I brought you here.

J. EDGAR HOOVER: If I may, Ma'am.

PALMER: Hoover…

EDITH: Go ahead, Mr. Hoover.

J. EDGAR HOOVER: Well, Ma'am. The Vice President's most famous quote to date is, "What this country needs is a really good five cent cigar."

Edith laughs.

J. EDGAR HOOVER: Rest assured, Ma'am. While Woodrow Wilson is lying on his broad back we will not be a party to having him ousted. The Reds are gathering steam since the Bolshevik revolution. Their forces are everywhere. We want to make sure, during his recovery, that the country remains safe. Ma'am. If Mr. Palmer can't speak to the President directly, we are fearful of what will become of America.

PALMER: Hoover; tell the First Lady your idea.

J. EDGAR HOOVER: Deportation.

EDITH: Deportation?

PALMER: A complete overturn of Immigration policy.

EDITH: And how will you accomplish this?

J. EDGAR HOOVER: By enacting the laws, Ma'am. And if the present laws don't cover our needs, we'll write new ones.

PALMER: We have been hunting for the evilest Red in the country to be the public face of our patriotic mission.

J. EDGER HOOVER: We will clean up America. On the President's watch.

PALMER: And the first to be deported will be the biggest fish in the radical sea. Go on, Son; tell the First Lady his name.

J. EDGAR HOOVER: Emma Goldman.

Pause.

PALMER: That's a woman's name, Hoover!

J. EDGAR HOOVER: Yes, Sir.

PALMER: A woman won't sell in the press. The public will feel sorry for her.

EDITH: Are you saying all a woman can evoke is pity Mr. Palmer? Tell me more about this Emma Goldman, Hoover.

J. EDGAR HOOVER: She's a radical anarchist, has disgusting views on birth control and free love. She's just been imprisoned for the last two years for publicly opposing the War. I have grown to hate her in just 24 hours, and I can make the rest of the country despise and fear her. I will call her "The Most Dangerous Woman In America"

EDITH: "The Most Dangerous Woman In America!" I like it.

PALMER: "The Most Dangerous Woman In America..."

EDITH: OK Palmer. You will see the President. The only member of his cabinet allowed entry. The President has suffered Thrombosis. He cannot sit up in bed or stop himself from drooling. He is paralyzed on his left side and blind in one eye. Once you have visited with him, you will tell the press that Woodrow Wilson is fine, recovering very well, will return to work shortly. Understood?

PALMER: Yes Ma'am.

EDITH: Are you ready?

PALMER: Now?

EDITH: Of course now. Wait here, Hoover. You will have your turn with the President one day. I've no doubt.

J. EDGAR HOOVER: Thank You, Ma'am.

Edith exits. Palmer turns to J. Edgar Hoover.

PALMER: Wait here.

Lights shift. Matron enters Emma's cell holding a package behind her back.

MATRON: Are you a homosexual?

EMMA: What?

MATRON: Answer the question, Goldman.

EMMA: Why? Are you lonely, Matron? Poor dear, don't you have a girlfriend of your own?

Matron slaps Emma.

EMMA: What will you do for entertainment when I get out of here?

MATRON: You'll go out make big trouble. Get in all the papers. And I'll say I knew her when.

EMMA: I think you like me.

MATRON: All the other prisoners are scared of me. No you.

EMMA: What are you hiding behind your back?

MATRON: Nothing.

EMMA: Is that package for me? Give it here!

MATRON: Am I your slave?

EMMA: Of course not.

The Matron throws the package to the floor.

EMMA: What's this?

MATRON: Open it.

Emma opens it. It is a suit of clothes.

EMMA: Who sent these?
MATRON: It arrived this morning. From Ben Reitman.
EMMA: What are these clothes for?
MATRON: For you to wear tomorrow when you walk out of here.
EMMA: Tomorrow?
MATRON: You gone deaf, Goldman?
EMMA: I'm getting out?
MATRON: Two months early. Good behavior.

Emma moves towards her.

MATRON: Back up!
EMMA: I only wanted to embrace you.
MATRON: You embrace me; I'll kick you to the floor.
EMMA: Thank you, Matron.
MATRON: Nothing to do with me. Just get to the showers before you put on them new duds. You stink like hell.

Matron turns to leave. Emma runs at her and hugs her from behind. Male Reporter enters.

MALE REPORTER: New York, 1919. Headline of the day: The 18th Amendment to the United States Constitution finally authorizes Prohibition.

Female reporter enters.

FEMALE REPORTER: Headline of the day: The 19th Amendment to the United States Constitution finally guarantees women the right to vote.

MALE REPORTER: Headline of the day: Rosa Luxemburg is murdered!
FEMALE REPORTER: Headline of the day: Einstein's theory of general relativity is confirmed by a total solar eclipse!
MALE REPORTER: On Broadway: Helen Keller, the famous deaf, blind and formally / dumb girl.
FEMALE REPORTER: On Broadway: An all-Yiddish production of Tevye / The Milkman.
FEMALE REPORTER and MALE REPORTER: New York, 1919
FEMALE REPORTER: After the Great War stops bleeding,
MALE REPORTER: Before the roaring twenties begin to roar,
FEMALE REPORTER: This old island is the new world.
MALE REPORTER: City of a conquering people
FEMALE REPORTER: Challenging London to be the center of the world.
MALE REPORTER: Here, you must dance wilder,
FEMALE REPORTER: Work harder,
MALE REPORTER: Drink deeper,
FEMALE REPORTER: Climb higher,
FEMALE REPORTER and MALE REPORTER: New York City.
MALE REPORTER: Midtown Manhattan. To be precise.
FEMALE REPORTER: Grand Central Station. To be exact.

Lights shift. Grand Central Station. Emma and Sasha see each other from across the room.

EMMA: Sasha?

He turns and stands up with effort. He has aged since she's seen him. A crutch supporting a ruined leg.

SASHA: Emma.
EMMA: Sashenka.
SASHA: You look good.
EMMA: I look old.

SASHA: I look terrible.
EMMA: You look like home.
SASHA: I can't even cross the distance been us on my own two feet.
EMMA: Then I will cross it.
SASHA: No! Stay there.
EMMA: Why?
SASHA: I don't want you to see me so weak. It's shameful how weak I am.
EMMA: You are the leader of a movement. You are the revolution incarnate. Bigger than the Rocky Mountains. Mightier than the Black Sea.
SASHA: I am tired.
EMMA: Two years in solitary is tiring.
SASHA: It broke me.
EMMA: You aren't broken. You are just torn a little.
SASHA: These two years were more pernicious than all the fourteen in Pennsylvania. I don't know why.
EMMA: Because despite the force of our rebel spirits, biology betrays us.
SASHA: We age.
EMMA: It creeps up.
SASHA: We wither.
EMMA: We creak.
SASHA: We wither.
EMMA: To change the world is not enough for us,
SASHA: The Revolution is no longer sufficient.
EMMA: We should rally our spirits to feed the poor
SASHA: Speak out for justice and freedom
EMMA: Lift up our shattered comrades
SASHA: The poor and disenfranchised
EMMA: The miners and the factory workers
SASHA: The political prisoners, the dead and dying
EMMA: But the cause is suddenly
SASHA: A hill too steep to climb?
EMMA: A river too wide to swim?

SASHA: We no longer dream about it.
EMMA: We dream of good wine.
SASHA: And sleep.
EMMA: Conversations with our dearest friend.
SASHA: The soft touch of our long lost lover.
EMMA: Warm bed, warm bath, chocolate cake.
SASHA: These fantasies are profane.
EMMA: They are terrible.
SASHA: We want to rest.
EMMA: Make love.
SASHA: To rest.
EMMA: No Sasha…
SASHA: We've given up.
EMMA: We must not give up. No. No. We go on.
SASHA: I don't know if I can go on, Emmela.
EMMA: You'll go on, Berkman. For the people.
SASHA: For the people, Goldman.
EMMA: Who are waiting for us now.
SAHSA: Who don't have the luxury of indolent daydreams.
EMMA: Or self-doubt.
SASHA: Or exhaustion.
EMMA: Who are counting on us.
SASHA: Counting on our fearless march towards freedom.
EMMA: They raised the money for our release.
SASHA: So we can pick up the torch of justice and fight on.
EMMA: With all the fire of newfound energy.
SASHA: We are the revolution incarnate.
EMMA: The leaders of a movement.
SASHA: Bigger than mountains.
EMMA: Mightier than seas.
SASHA: Roll up our sleeves, then.
EMMA: So much to be done.
SASHA: Start right away.
EMMA: Chicago.
SASHA: San Francisco.

EMMA: Baltimore.
SASHA: Pittsburgh.
EMMA: Boston.
SASHA: Minneapolis. Detroit.
EMMA: We won't stop until the wrongs are righted.
SASHA: Until the workers of the world unite in liberty.
EMMA: Until liberty is unrestricted by man-made law.
SASHA: Until America is herself again.
EMMA: No matter how many times they lock us up.
SASHA: No matter how tired or crippled.
EMMA: No matter how old.
SASHA: The first stop on our tour:
EMMA AND SASHA: New York.
EMMA: Union Square.
SASHA: You'll speak first, and I will follow.
EMMA: Together, we'll be young again.
SASHA: Together, we'll answer the call.
EMMA: Together, we can do anything.
SASHA: Comrade.
EMMA: I have missed you.
SASHA: Come here.

Emma walks slowly to him. He takes her face in his hands. Lights shift. A Hall. Alice and J. Edgar Hoover enter from opposite sides of the stage.

ALICE: Hello, Mr. Hoover.
J. EDGAR HOOVER: Alice, thank you for coming!
ALICE: Welcome to New York.
J. EDGAR HOOVER: Welcome to Sodom. Where the hell are we?
ALICE: A hall where the Reds gather. Goldman was scheduled to speak here tonight. But of course you have shut her down. Perhaps Berkman will take to the stage.
J. EDGAR HOOVER: Get me a table at the back of the room as usual, Alice. Where we won't be seen.

ALICE: Yes. Sir. Then I will meet you back at headquarters.

J. EDGAR HOOVER: No! Stay, Alice. I don't want to be left alone here.

ALICE: Sir?

J. EDGAR HOOVER: It's not that I'm afraid of them.

ALICE: No Sir.

J. EDGAR HOOVER: I am actually enjoying this, Alice. I find it disgusting. The filth, the sex, the noise, the Jews. But to be in the very halls with Berkman and Goldman. It's like being at the same saloon as Jesse James and John Wesley Harding. I'm a gunslinger too.

ALICE: Very brave, Sir.

J. EDGAR HOOVER: All in the line of duty Alice. All in the line. Where is your Husband?

ALICE: He's at the hotel, Sir. He ships out in the morning. He is glad that there are no hard feelings.

J. EDGAR HOOVER: No hard feelings about what? Listen Alice I need every single slip of paper on Emma Goldman and Alexander Berkman. We cannot miss anything. I promised Palmer, I'd build a case so strong it would hold up in any court in the nation.

ALICE: She has a lot of friends, Sir. Protecting her privacy.

J. EDGAR HOOVER: Be a snake Alice. Slither between rocks and turn them over.

ALICE: I have Sir. I've gone everywhere. In Rochester, her 80-year-old Mother shouts from her third floor window "You will never catch my daughter the great Emma Goldman!" The agents told her to be quiet, but she screamed. "If the United States Government can't stop my daughter from speaking, a fine chance you have of getting me to shut / up!"

J. EDGAR HOOVER: Shhhh! Here they come.

Emma and Sasha take the stage.

SASHA: Ladies and Gentlemen, we were told that Emma Goldman cannot speak here tonight.

The audience boos.

J. EDGAR HOOVER: My doing.

Sasha ties a gag over Emma's mouth.

SASHA: Because Emma cannot speak tonight we shall speak for her.
J. EDGAR HOOVER: She is ridiculous! A woman her age! Like a clown!
SASHA: Last night a group of policemen stormed the Russian People's House on East 15th Street. They forced the entire group to stand up and sing The Star Spangled Banner. At gunpoint.

The audience Boos.

J. EDGAR HOOVER: Did you hear that Alice?
ALICE: Yes Sir. It's working.
SASHA: We've been notified that The American Justice Department wants Emma Goldman and Alexander Berkman off its shores. They want us bound and gagged. Herded like cows to slaughter.

Boos.

J. EDGAR HOOVER: Goldman looks like a fool up there in her little vaudeville pantomime.
SASHA: Do we bow our heads and offer up our hands to their chains? Or do we fight the laws, pouring out of Washington, a new law each week – laws that aim to keep our good voices silent?

Boos

J. EDGAR HOOVER: Fight the laws? Who do they think they are?
ALICE: They are certainly not Patriots Sir.

J. EDGAR HOOVER: They are anti-patriot terrorists. These people must be stopped
SASHA: Ladies and Gentleman. Shall I remove Emma Goldman's gag?

The audience Cheers

J. EDGAR HOOVER: No!

Sasha removes Emma's gag.

EMMA: What is Patriotism, Ladies and Gentlemen?
Nothing more than the adoration of a spot.
The Spot of birthplace.
Mother's knee. Memory.
Patriotism is childhood's call
To love the place we threw a ball,
The patch of green, the front porch swing
Where we'd sit and dream and the birds would sing.
Is that patriotism? If it is we are in deep trouble.
Because so many Americans will shudder
To discover
Their spot of youth
Is now a factory, mine, or mill?
And the music of the birds is now the shrill
Whine of machinery grinding out
Patriotism.
J. EDGAR HOOVER: Put the gag back on!
EMMA: Some have the fortune of being born and raised
On some particular spot that is more highly praised.
Its people are nobler, grander, of more worth
Than those inhabiting humbler spots on earth.
It is, therefore, the civic duty
Of all living on that spot of beauty
To fight, kill, die, lie, cheat and bribe

To save superior folk from inferior tribes.
From infancy on, a child's innocent brain
Is poisoned with such cultural disdain.
And when the child is grown, it's his belief
He's been chosen by God /to shield his spot from grief:
The invasion by foreigners.
J.EDGAR HOOVER: Shut that woman up!
EMMA: "Patriotism justifies the training of wholesale murderers",
    says Leo Tolstoy, himself not such a patriotic / boy.
J.EDGAR HOOVER: Alice, I can't take much more of her!
EMMA: Those of us who were not born here
Inspire True Patriots with a deadly / fear
J.EDGAR HOOVER: Her voice grates on me!
EMMA: For the ultimate purity of this good nation,
They build up their force of secret agents
Who hide at back tables, a security mob?
Scaring us out of stealing/ American jobs.
J.EDGAR HOOVER: Enough! Go on Alice./ Get my men.

Alice exits.

EMMA: America is the holiest spot, the golden ring.
Everyone will stand to salute and sing.
At gunpoint. Ladies and Gentlemen.
Such is the logic of Patriotism.
J. EDGAR HOOVER: SHUT IT DOWN!

Lights up on Reporters.

FEMALE REPORTER and MALE REPORTER: The Palmer Raids.
FEMALE REPORTER: At 9 p.m. November 7, 1919, a date chosen because it is the second anniversary of the Bolshevik revolution,
MALE REPORTER: Agents of the Bureau of Investigation, led by Attorney General Mitchell Palmer

J. EDGAR HOOVER: But secretly organized and implemented by J. Edgar Hoover.

EMMA: Execute a series of violent raids against innocent people.

FEMALE REPORTER: Government agents cast a wide net, bringing in Russians

MALE REPORTER: And some passers-by who admitted to being immigrants.

SASHA*: Teachers who just happened to be conducting night school classes!

MALE REPORTER: Criminals and terrorists bent on destroying America

EMMA: Hundreds are arrested.

SASHA*: Dragged out of apartments and meeting halls.

FEMALE REPORTER: The police are joined by a volunteer band of soldiers and sailors all shouting-

EMMA AND SASHA*: GO HOME RED!

MALE REPORTER: The Raids continue throughout the city.

EMMA: In Restaurants.

SASHA*: In Schools. Meeting halls.

FEMALE REPORTER: At Dance concerts. Where terrorist deviants such as

Isadora Duncan!

MALE REPORTER: Close friend to Emma Goldman.

FEMALE REPORTER: Is dancing to the Internationale in a long red dress.

SASHA*: Many Russians are critically injured. Some die.

EMMA: Babies die!

MALE REPORTER: 650 are arrested and brought to Ellis Island for deportation.

FEMALE REPORTER: Palmer reports that his department had amassed 60,000 more immigrant names.

J. EDGAR HOOVER: Names actually accumulated by J. Edgar Hoover.

Lights shift. Emma and J. EDGAR HOOVER in two spotlights.

EMMA: Comrades. Fight back. / We are everywhere!

J. EDGAR HOOVER: Reds are everywhere! The street are teeming with evil. Hiding in sewers, in cupboards and closets, /in mirrors, under rocks.
EMMA: The Romanovs have been hurled from their thrones! The Tsar is gone. Russia is free! / Stand up and Join us!
J. EDGAR HOOVER: Our country is at risk. We must maintain law and order. These Reds are not American/ they are disguised as yourself, as your countrymen. But look closely-
EMMA: I am an American in the truest sense, spiritually rather than by the grace of a mere scrap of paper/
J. EDGAR HOOVER: We must now face the harsh truth that the objectives of communism/ are being steadily advanced.
EMMA: For 30 years I have lived, dreamed and worked for the America I love. For the America/ whose physical grandeur and beauty and freedom promised me life!
J. EDGAR HOOVER: The individual is handicapped by a Conspiracy so monstrous he cannot believe it exists. / The American mind has not come to a realization of the evil, which has been introduced into our midst.
EMMA: When Wilson's decision to push the US to join the European slaughter to make the world safe for democracy/ America has drifted into dark waters. And now
J. EDGAR HOOVER: America is now the prime target of international communism. And nowhere is innocence more drowned/ than in America.
EMMA: America is drowning.
J.EDGAR HOOVER: I watch from the shadows. Ready to pounce. / She starts up again.
EMMA: Friends! We must resist a government that insists on this violent wave of tyranny!
J. EDGAR HOOVER: I've had agents covering every stop / Tonight they are ready. I give the order.
EMMA: DEFEAT OUR ENEMIES IN THIS NOBLE FIGHT.
J.EDGAR HOOVER: The police descend on Emma Goldman. / I CATCH MY FISH!

EMMA: Sasha!

The police grab Emma and Sasha drag them offstage. Lights shift. Ellis Island.

FEMALE REPORTER: Ellis Island. Deportation Hearing. The United States versus Emma Goldman.

JUDGE: What is your legal name?

EMMA: Emma Goldman Kersner

JUDGE: What name do you use now?

EMMA: Emma Goldman.

JUDGE: Miss Goldman, The Anarchist Exclusion Act states that "Any alien who entertains a belief in the overthrow of the Government of the United States is subject to immediate deportation."

EMMA: I am citizen by marriage.

JUDGE: Where is your husband?

EMMA: I have not seen Jacob Kersner for ten years.

J. EDGAR HOOVER: We have found Jacob Kersner, Your Honor and he's dead in New Jersey.

EMMA GOLDMAN: But we are still married. He had his citizenship.

JUDGE: Miss Goldman, are you an anarchist?

EMMA: I decline to answer.

JUDGE*: Mr. Berkman, are you an anarchist?

SASHA*: I decline to answer.

JUDGE: Miss Goldman, you deny being an anarchist?

EMMA: I decline to answer.

JUDGE*: Mr. Berkman?

SASHA*: I decline to answer.

J. EDGAR HOOVER: EMMA GOLDMAN AND ALEXANDER BERKMAN ARE BEYOND DOUBT TWO OF THE MOST BLOODTHIRSTY ANARCHISTS IN THIS COUNTRY!

EMMA: Who is this J. Edgar Hoover?? My newest enemy. So virulent and so angry. So handsome and so young. I've seen him before.

He's the fellow in the hat in the back of every room we've spoken in for the last few weeks.

Lights shift. The Library of Congress. J. Edgar and Alice.

J. EDGAR: Where is Don?
ALICE: He's in the closet.
J. EDGAR: He's where?
ALICE: He's in trouble with the bosses. They put him on filing.
J. EDGAR: Why is he in trouble?
ALICE: I don't know, Mr. Hoover.
J. EDGAR: Get him out here.

She hurries off. J. Edgar Hoover paces. Don enters.

DON: Mr. Hoover.
J. EDGAR HOOVER: They giving you trouble, Don?
DON: Nothing I can't handle.
J. EDGAR HOOVER: Is it because of me?
DON: Don't worry about it.
J. EDGAR HOOVER: I need a favor.
DON: You know I'd do anything for you.
J. EDGAR HOOVER: This is big stuff, Don. This involves THE PRESIDENT OF THE UNITED STATES.
DON: You don't have to scare me.
J. EDGAR HOOVER: I need help slicing a fish.
DON: Slicing?
J. EDGAR HOOVER: A big fish.
DON: Emma Goldman.
J. EDGAR HOOVER: You've been following my work.
DON: I follow your every move.
J. EDGAR HOOVER: You do?
DON: I have something for you. Something you'll like.
J. EDGAR HOOVER: What?
DON: It's about a Jewish "Rabie".

J. EDGAR HOOVER: Rabbi.
DON: Well this particular Ribeye was not ordained properly in New York State.
J. EDGAR HOOVER: So?
DON: This is the fellow that married Emma Goldman to her husband. And she is claiming citizenship based on that marriage, so if-
J. EDGAR HOOVER: So if the Rabbi wasn't ordained in the eyes of the state, the marriage is null and void, so is Goldman's claim of citizenship! I could kiss you Don.
DON: Why don't you?

Don steps towards J. Edgar Hoover, who steps back.

J. EDGAR HOOVER
Don. Listen to me carefully. If you ever leak even one tiny hint about anything that ever happened between us-
DON: I love you.
J. EDGAR HOOVER: Shut your fucking mouth.

Lights shift. The Ellis Island court. The Judge reads:

JUDGE: As the acting commissioner of immigration, I do hereby find due to the lack of the Rabbi's valid licensure, that Emma Goldman's marriage is null and void. She is therefore a non-citizen. By the authority vested in me, I do hereby command this court to return the said alien to Russia, the country from whence she came.
EMMA: Such a tiny small thing. A Rabbi's license?
J. EDGAR HOOVER The order for deportation is signed!
EMMA: THESE PROCEEDINGS ARE A REVIVAL OF CZARIST RUSSIA. EVER SINCE I HAVE BEEN IN THIS COUNTRY, I HAVE BEEN TAUGHT THAT ONE IS FREE TO THINK AND FEEL AS HE PLEASES. / WHAT BECOMES OF THIS SACRED GUARANTEE OF FREEDOM WHEN PEOPLE ARE BEING PERSECUTED AND DRIVEN OUT FOR THE VERY

MOTIVES FOR WHICH THE PIONEERS WHO BUILT THIS COUNTRY LAID DOWN THEIR LIVES?
J. EDGAR HOOVER: SHUT HER UP!
JUDGE: I AM WARNING YOU, MISS GOLDMAN!
EMMA: SASHA!
JUDGE: THEY WILL BE HELD AT ELLIS ISLAND TO AWAIT DEPORTATION.
SASHA*: Prison again, Emma.
EMMA: Prison again, Comrade.
J. EDGAR HOOVER: We have won, Mr. Palmer! We have won! The fish is hooked!

Lights shift. Emma, alone in her cell. Margaret Sanger enters in a big hat pulled down over her face.

EMMA: Margaret Sanger!

Emma points to Margaret's hat.

EMMA: Are you in disguise?
MARGARET: There are reporters everywhere.
EMMA: You don't want them to see you paying a last visit to an old friend? You wouldn't come visit me in Missouri.
MARGARET: I'm here now.
EMMA: And I am grateful.
MARGARET: I can't stay long. I am speaking to a group at the New York Athletic club tonight on birth control.
EMMA: Why not broaden your scope, Margaret? A few years ago you I gave you a taste of the labor movement, remember? The factory strike.
MARGARET: You were my mentor once. But I have grown up. A socialist revolution is not the most effective way to improve conditions for women.
EMMA: Birth Control is best viewed as part of the larger issue the fight against POVERTY AND INJUSTICE.

MARGARET: THIS is my issue.

EMMA: Perhaps, burdened by the success of one cause, you are overlooking the ethics of the big picture.

MARGARET: I am working with scientists to produce a chemical, which will kill sperm on contact. One day an oral contraceptive will be developed that women can be take like aspirin.

EMMA: We must make all these wonderful inventions useful for the working classes.

MARGARET: Rich women in Connecticut need help as much as tenement girls on the Lower East Side.

EMMA: You know as well as I that the rich will always be able to find and pay for medical care.

MARGARET: I have made a new start, new platform-

EMMA: New friends?

MARGARET: I need to separate from the image of my past, from-

EMMA: Anarchists and revolutionaries?

MARGARET: My cause needs funding and I have found the women to fund it.

EMMA: Yes I've heard about your Committee of 100 with their fur coats and private drivers. You've come a long way from wanting to relieve poor women with swords hanging over their heads!

MARGARET: I DON'T OWE YOU A THING. NOT JUSTIFICATION, NOT EXPLANATION. NOT EVEN CONVERSATION!

EMMA: YOU WOULD BE NOWHERE WITHOUT ME!

MARGARET: YOU ARE JEALOUS! YOUR FIGURE STARTED TO GO AND THE MEN STARTED TO CIRCLE AROUND ME INSTEAD. I AM YOUNGER, THINNER, BRIGHTER, AND LESS DOGMATIC.

Pause.

MARGARET (CONT'D): Why did you want to see me?

EMMA: A very eager young department of Justice official named J. Edgar Hoover will have Sasha and me on a boat to Russia in less than two weeks if we can't raise money for another appeal. Perhaps you'll help, old friend.

MARGARET: It's not safe to help you and Berkman. The Government has been investigating me too.

EMMA: According to Hoover I'm "the most dangerous woman in America."

MARGARET: I thought I was.

EMMA: Dubious competition, Margaret. We are asking our friends to do everything they can. We don't want to be forced out of our home.

MARGARET: America isn't your home.

EMMA: What is home? When I was younger, the cause was my home. When we were out on the road you and Ben and me, fighting for birth control home was wherever we laid our heads. I loved my little place on 13th street, but it was never the walls and bookshelves I needed. Just the words inside the books. I once told you all I needed to withstand prison was a good book. Do you remember? Sasha is my home. We never needed more than our work and the knowledge that while one of us was giving a speech or marching, the other one was somewhere else even in jail, doing the same thing. We came to this country, reveled in its beauty and we have worked tirelessly to build it into a nation of justice. But as they try to push me out the door I realize that, now that I am fifty years old, I need a harbor and a gathering place. America is my home, Margaret. Please help me stay.

MARGARET: There is nothing I can do to help you. Your goose is cooked, Emma. The story of your life here has come to an end.

EMMA: You won't be sad to see me go.

MARGARET: You'll be better off in Russia. The revolution is there. I must go. I am due at the Athletic Club.

EMMA: An institution, which does not admit Jews or Blacks.

MARGARET: Goodbye, Emma.

Margaret STANDS and turns to exit.

EMMA: Margaret!
MARGARET: Yes?
EMMA: Be careful. Ambition can be dangerous to your soul.
MARGARET: Yes, Emma, you should know.

She exits.

EMMA: I am ambitious for the movement, for the cause. Not for myself….

Lights come up on J. Edgar Hoover writing a letter.

J. EDGAR HOOVER: Mr. Palmer, I am putting out fires every day: Fire #1: I found a boat. It's old, a "Sea roller", the liberals around Ellis Island are trying to grind me to a halt saying that it's "inhumane transport". They say the Buford is not seaworthy. Storm seasons in the icy North Sea, etc. But I forge ahead. Fire #2: Silence Strikes – 80 immigrants from the raids are taken to Ellis Island. They are told they have the right to a lawyer. They all hire the same one. A Jew from the National Civil Liberties Bureau. He tells them to stop answering to their names so we can't tell who is who. Fire #3: Hunger strike. The immigrants stop eating. I say, "Let them starve!" Fire #4: A visitor sneaks a small camera in. I have security tightened. Fire #5: The children. The REDS say they have kids born on American soil, which makes them citizens. They don't want to be separated from the offspring. This one I keep away from the press. But damn if Goldman and Berkman don't try to start up Fire #6.

Lights up on Ellis Island.

SASHA: We are not here to start a fire. Comrades, we are here to speak to you as friends who know your sorrow. There are hundreds of us immigrants imprisoned here. We know it is not easy to say goodbye.

EMMA: One does not live in a country for over 30 years live as we have lived and find it easy to go. We found our spiritual birth here. All the turmoil of body and soul, all the love, and all the hate that come to an intense human being in a lifetime, have come to us in this country.
SASHA: Perhaps comrades we will meet again in a free Russia.
EMMA: Where we'll find more fertile ground for our ideals.
SASHA: Nonetheless it is hard to say goodbye.
EMMA: I fought and fought against leaving but then I realized: If Sasha is to be driven out of the country, I will go too. It is unthinkable that he join the revolution without me.
SASHA: So to the thousands who have been held, are being held, will be held here on Ellis Island
EMMA: We offer you our strength and our love
SASHA: Do not be sad about our forced departure.
EMMA: Rather rejoice with us in the knowledge that our common enemies have resorted to this mad act because they have heard our shouts and they are afraid.
SASHA: This is our farewell to you. The light of Liberty burns low just now. But do not despair, friends. Soon there will come a rift in the darkness and the New Day will break even in this country. May each of us feel that we have contributed toward the great Awakening. Be brave.

Lights shift.

EMMA: Very early one morning.
J. EDGAR HOOVER: December 21st, 1919.
EMMA: On the coldest day of the year

Two guards enter.

MALE GUARD: WAKE UP!
EMMA: We are shaken awake at three o'clock in the morning. It is dark. We don't understand at first what is happening.

MALE GUARD: Get up now! Get your things!

FEMALE GUARD: Hurry, there! Hurry!

EMMA: They are pushing us down long dark corridors chilled by freezing winter winds. Little messenger boys running around with last minute 'telegrams" scribbled on slips of paper to wives, lawyers, friends, children they'll never see again.

MALE GUARD: MARCH.

FEMALE GUARD: GO!

EMMA: Through deep snow from the dormitory through the iced air to the gangplank of the barge./ We stand at the harbor shivering.

J. EDGAR HOOVER: I invite some of my agents to accompany me to Battery Park and onto the ferry to Ellis Island. / I savor my greatest victory.

MALE REPORTER: 249 prisoners of the Ellis Island detention facility

FEMALE REPORTER: Are herded to a barge. Which will transport them to a The Buford. Anchored out in the middle of New York harbor.

J. EDGAR HOOVER: I have maps of Russia, Finland, and Latvia, so I can study the vacation our anarchist friends/ are taking.

EMMA: We file past the dignitaries and government officials in their fur / coats.

J. EDGAR HOOVER: A group of us stand proudly in our winter / coats.

EMMA: A mob is a mob, even if it is from the Department of/ Justice.

J. EDGAR HOOVER: The mood is jovial. We joke: The Soviet Ark will be America's Christmas present to Lenin and Trotsky. / Ha-ha.

EMMA: They are laughing at us.

J. EDGAR HOOVER: Emma Goldman thumbs her nose at us from a distance as they load her onto the barge. Merry Christmas, Emma!

EMMA: We are about to be cast off American/ soil.

J. EDGAR HOOVER: Soldiers armed with a rifles and pistols/ are on guard.

EMMA: Sasha is dressed like a Cossack soldier/ with a long cravat.

J. EDGAR HOOVER: Goldman carries her battered typewriter/ under one arm.

EMMA: Hoover is standing there, grinning and gloating. He is the only thing I am happy to be rid of.

J. EDGAR HOOVER At the last moment, I decide to board the barge and accompany the criminals to the ship.

Emma Goldman is sitting in the belly of the barge looking out at the New York skyline. J. Edgar Hoover enters. He doesn't expect to see her there.

EMMA: J. Edgar Hoover.

J. EDGAR HOOVER: Emma Goldman.

EMMA: At long last. Face to face.

J. EDGAR HOOVER: It doesn't seem appropriate to shake hands.

EMMA: No point in pretending.

J. EDGAR HOOVER: Didn't intend to disturb you. I thought you were with Berkman and the others.

EMMA: I came down here for warmth and solitude in my last few minutes of America.

J. EDGAR HOOVER: I'll go back up then.

He shivers, pulling his coat tight.

EMMA: You are cold.

J. EDGAR HOOVER: It is windy on deck.

EMMA: You chose a frigid moment for your act of vengeance.

J. EDGAR HOOVER: Act of Patriotism, Miss Goldman.

EMMA: Late December, middle of the night. It's clever, actually. A proper send off for treacherous insurgents, humbled by shivering.

J. EDGAR HOOVER: You'll be docking in Finland and making the final trek through frozen Russian fields. I imagine the pre-dawn New York harbor will seem balmy in comparison.

EMMA: True.

J. EDGAR HOOVER: The hour of departure is perfect. You'll be gone before the day dawns and you are able to darken another American morning.

EMMA: You have accomplished your mission.

J. EDGAR HOOVER: This is the proudest day of my life.

EMMA: Ah.

J. EDGAR HOOVER: I am deporting 249 of the most violent anarchist criminals.

EMMA: Most of the people on this barge believe in nothing more than a "theoretical anarchism" and have never participated in a single act of violence in their lives.

J. EDGAR HOOVER: Claim what you will, Goldman. We are cleansing our country of you.

EMMA: If you cleanse the land that once held its arms open to the world, you'll have to change the inscription on the Statue of Liberty. It should say: " Bring me your tired, your poor, I will spit on them."

J. EDGAR HOOVER: I wonder if Lenin will be able to shut you up. If it wasn't so cold out there I wouldn't tolerate your blathering one more minute.

EMMA: But aren't you afraid?

J. EDGAR HOOVER: Afraid of what?

EMMA: Of being alone with "The Most Dangerous Woman in America"?

J. EDGAR HOOVER: There are 68-armed military men onboard this barge.

EMMA: You'll need 68-armed men to subdue a 50-year-old woman.

J. EDGAR HOOVER: In a few hours' time you'll have passed over the borders of this nation, and believe me, I'll dedicate my life to making sure you never come back again.

EMMA: You are a very dedicated young man. You ruin lives with reverent alacrity.

J. EDGAR HOOVER: I don't know what you're complaining about. You're going home to the Bolsheviks. You can join the revolution.

EMMA: I joined the revolution, Mr. Hoover, long before you were born.

J. EDGAR HOOVER: Thank God you are not an American, and your revolutionist agitation is no longer my problem.

EMMA: I've lived in America 34 years. That's longer than you've been alive. Which I guess makes me more American than you.

J. EDGAR HOOVER: You've criticized this country from the moment you got here.

EMMA: I have never criticized her people. Only her government. America is the hobos on trains in the west and the miners coughing black blood in the east. The pregnant women on the lower east side, the workers in the garment industry sweat shops. America is made up of people that you don't even want to see. I love America.

J. EDGAR HOOVER: You show it by inciting riots? You are a terrorist and America will be much better off without you.

EMMA: This is the beginning of the end for this country. There will be more war, more poverty. This country will fail as the old Russia did. With Tsars like you at the helm.

J. EDGAR HOOVER: As long as we keep the RED out of the red, white and blue, we'll do just fine.

EMMA: Without the red, what have you got, Mr. Hoover? Greece?

J. EDGAR HOOVER: Do you think you are a comedian, Miss Goldman? Will that be your new profession now that you're public speaking career is over?

EMMA: A broken ship skulks away at 4:00 a.m. Immigrants and citizens torn from their beds in the dead of night and pushed away from shore before lawyers and the press can shine a light on your treachery, before wives and mothers can bring blankets and coats, before children can say goodbye. You are the terrorist, not me.

J. EDGAR HOOVER: You are finished, Miss Goldman.

EMMA: You are young, Mr. Hoover.

J. EDGAR HOOVER: You hate me for winning. You'll write about me in your speeches for years to come.

EMMA: I will not write one word about you as long as I live.

J. EDGAR HOOVER: I don't believe you.

EMMA: Believe me, I will not waste my ink on your name nor will I contribute to the infamy you are sure to attain. I won't waste my heart.

J. EDGAR HOOVER: You've wasted your heart on a lot of men. Did you ever charge money for it? Because you certainly have behaved like a whore.

EMMA: Let me ask you something, John Edgar Hoover. Or should I call you John? Or Edgar. Or J. E.?

J. EDGAR HOOVER: Call me Sir.

EMMA: J.E. Who broke you and made you such an angry little man? I'll bet it was your father. Was it your father?

J. EDGAR HOOVER: SHUT UP!

EMMA: I hit a nerve.

J. EDGAR HOOVER: I'll call one of the guards to lock you to the railing!

EMMA: Tell me about your father, J.E.

J. EDGAR HOOVER: Don't call me that!

EMMA: You are what, 24 years old? Well dressed. Well educated. No doubt you will grow into a formidable opponent. But right now all I see is a little man in a fancy suit who on the proudest day of his life has accomplished nothing. You are small potatoes, J.E.

J. EDGAR HOOVER: I AM ALL THE POTATOES, MISS GOLDMAN. I AM SOLELY RESPONSIBLE FOR THE REMOVAL OF NEARLY 300 COMMUNISTS! I WAS BEHIND THE PALMER RAIDS! I AM RESCUING AMERICA! AND THE FIGHT IS JUST BEGINNING. I AM A FORCE TO BE RECKONED WITH! YOU WAIT AND SEE! PALMER TOOK ALL THE CREDIT. BUT THOSE WERE NOT THE PALMER RAIDS – THEY WERE THE HOOVER RAIDS. MY RAIDS,

MY SHIP! MY COMMUNISTS, MINE! AND YOU BETTER REMEMBER THAT. GO TO HELL!

EMMA: Or to Finland, whichever comes first.

J. EDGAR HOOVER: I hate you more than I have ever hated anyone.

EMMA: I don't believe you really hate me that much.

J. EDGAR HOOVER: "As a foe, the anarchist is fearless only of his own life, for his creed is the creed of the criminal mind."

EMMA: You are quoting the Attorney General.

J. EDGER HOOVER: My mentor.

EMMA: You aren't as genuinely bloodthirsty for Anarchists as Mr. Palmer. You took on his mission because it served your ambition. You were in the wrong place at the wrong time.

J. EDGAR HOOVER
You don't know anything about me.

EMMA: I think we know each other very well. Enemies always do. Your deepest desire is not protecting the country from Reds; your true passion is something else.

J. EDGER HOOVER: My true passion?

EMMA: Spying on people, Mr. Hoover. You think I didn't see you in the back room of every speech I gave? You think I don't know the hours you poured into research, tracking my every statement, my every friend, my every single move?

J. EDGAR HOOVER: I believe in my work.

EMMA: You don't believe in anything! I wake up with my beliefs. When I take a drink I remember those in prison with nothing but dirty water. When I take a bite of food, I think of Joe Hill in front of the firing squad shouting "don't mourn for me, organize!" When I put my shoes on, I think of the four Haymarket martyrs who were killed for crimes they did not commit. All you believe in is your credentials.

J. EDGAR HOOVER: I will not let you speak to me this way!

EMMA: But I am speaking to you this way. And you won't leave or stop me or have me locked to the railing of the ship. Because something in my words is ringing true.

J. EDGAR HOOVER: I feel sorry for you! I have a mother around your age, and I suppose if you had been able to have children you might have a son my age. I pity you for ending up like this.

EMMA: That was a low blow, Mr. Hoover.

J. EDGAR HOOVER: You have an inverted womb. So even though you had hundreds of chances with hundreds of men you could never have babies and if you did it would perhaps have mellowed you and made you less of a beast and more of a woman.

EMMA: You are more cruel than I imagined, young man.

J. EDGAR HOOVER: I did alright by you; I gave you a square deal.

EMMA: A square deal?

J. EDGAR HOOVER: If I put you away for treason, you'd never get out.

You should be grateful to me that you escaped the electric chair. You should thank me.

EMMA: No you should thank me. I am your first political victory. It's like your first love. You will build your career on this very morning. I deserve some gift in return.

J. EDGAR HOOVER: What gift?

EMMA: Tell me a secret, Mr. Hoover.

J. EDGAR HOOVER: Don't be ridiculous.

EMMA: You owe me at least one.

J. EDGAR HOOVER: A confidence? That's what you want? You think I should trust my secrets to a sworn enemy?

EMMA: Why not?

J. EDGAR HOOVER: You are a witch.

EMMA: I am a priest. Confess your sins to me and leave this barge a free man.

J. EDGAR HOOVER: You're insane.

EMMA: We're nearing the Buford. 249 souls will exit your life forever. Then where will you be? Without a sworn enemy.

J. EDGAR HOOVER: Don't flatter yourself. I'll find others.

EMMA: You have only a few minutes to speak the truth. You know you want to tell me.

J. EDGAR HOOVER: I could tell you anything I wanted. Your voice will be drowned out by waves, and even if you reach far off Russia and say anything, no one would ever believe you.

EMMA: So you have nothing to lose. Be brave. Are you brave?

He whispers something in her ear.

EMMA Congratulations. You've concealed the facts with a vengeance.

He whispers something else. She laughs.

EMMA: Well hooray for you, Mr. Hoover. So do I.

J. EDGAR HOOVER: And no one will ever know.

EMMA: Do you want me to absolve you of your sins?

J. EDGAR HOOVER: There are no sins, Miss Goldman.

EMMA: Just secrets, Mr. Hoover.

J. EDGAR HOOVER: Five fathoms deep.

EMMA: You could have been a great person. If only you hadn't run into Mitchell Palmer when your ambition was at its peak. You are a smart and passionate young man. You could have been a revolutionary.

J. EDGAR HOOVER: Not likely.

EMMA: Have you read Gorki's prose poem "the Snake and The Falcon"?

J. EDGAR HOOVER: I don't read Russian.

EMMA: The snake says to the falcon: "Why don't you rest here in the dark, in the good warm, safe, slimy moisture? Why fly to the heavens? Don't you know the dangers lurking there, the storms, the hunter's gun?" But the falcon pays no heed; it spreads its wings and soars. One day the falcon is brought down by a hunter, blood streaming from its heart, and the snake says: "You fool, I warned you, I told you to stay where I am, in the dark, where no one could find you." With its last breath the falcon says: " But I have soared through space, beheld the light, I have lived. I have lived."

J. EDGAR HOOVER: I am the snake and you the falcon?

EMMA: It's not too late to choose flight.

J. EDGAR HOOVER: We are born as we are.

EMMA: Are we?

J. EDGAR HOOVER: Have you changed at all in 50 years?

EMMA: I think I have. I used to blow things up. Dance wildly. Fall into love with a terrible crash. I used to hate everyone who disagreed with me.

J. EDGAR HOOVER: And now?

EMMA: Now I am sitting here with you.

Emma looks out at the harbor.

EMMA: Look! There she is. I remember my first glimpse of her.

J. EDGAR HOOVER: Must have been quite a sight.

EMMA: The way my sister and I stood and wept the day we arrived in America. The entire Russian population was on deck, staring out at her. The Captain begged everyone to move as the whole ship was listing to one side. But no one would budge.

J. EDGAR HOOVER: "Here at our sea-washed, sunset gates shall stand. A mighty woman with a torch,"

EMMA: "Whose flame is the imprisoned lightning,"

J. EDGAR HOOVER: "And her name Mother of Exiles."

EMMA: Your mother will be proud of you today.

J. EDGAR HOOVER: Your mother is proud too. She shouts out the window about her famous daughter.

EMMA: I will never see my Mother again.

J. EDGAR HOOVER: About that one fact, I am truly sorry.

EMMA: I'd like to be alone now.

J. EDGAR HOOVER: Goodbye, Emma Goldman.

He exits. Lights fade out on Emma.

MALE REPORTER: The Buford steams off at 4:20 am into the darkness with 52 anarchists 184 members of the Union of Russian Workers, one pimp, three aliens with lose morals and a man who got into the country surreptitiously.

FEMALE REPORTER: Mitchell Palmer issues a statement:

PALMER: It is hoped and expected that other vessels, larger, carrying similar cargoes, will follow in her wake."

FEMALE REPORTER: Emma's friends and lovers write letters:

BEN: Now you are in far off Russia, Little Mommy. Exiled but not isolated. Deported, but not cast out. You will come back. America is big and beautiful and when she awakens to your usefulness she will welcome you home.

FEMALE REPORTER: But Emma Goldman was never welcomed back to America.

Only once more in her life was she allowed re-entry to The United States. For a 90 day lecture tour on the social significance of the drama.

J. Edgar Hoover enters.

J. EDGAR HOOVER: I go on to become a famous American hero, heading the Federal Bureau of Investigation under five Presidents. The unsubstantiated rumors that I am a biracial cross dressing homosexual only increase the power of my legacy. Red Emma however is long forgotten.

FEMALE REPORTER: Today in Boston a woman read her autobiography and thought she is just like me, if I were brave

MALE REPORTER: Today in Detroit a man realized: if she spent all that time in prison for her ideals I can at least stand up to my supervisor.

FEMALE REPORTER: Today in Minneapolis a factory worker marched on a picket line carrying her picture on a stick.

MALE REPORTER: Today in Philadelphia a college student spoke at a May Day rally in memory of her.

FEMALE REPORTER: Today in San Francisco a teenage girl wrote a play about her.
MALE REPORTER: Today in St. Louis a professor penned her into a history book.
FEMALE REPORTER: Today when I was lost and fearful, I heard her voice.

Emma runs on.

EMMA: You over there with your head down in the program! You over there concealing your blush with a paper fan! WAKE UP! It is time to cry LOVE and cry PEACE and cry NOW.

Blackout. End Of Play.

NOBODY IS SLEEPING

By Jessica Litwak

Setting: 1936-1940.
Setting: 1936-1940.

The set needs to be flexible and become, among other places: A battlefield, a prison, a Spanish street and a Scottish lecture hall. This is true ensemble that recreates a revolution. The collage of characters are each identified by specific vocal and physical choices (accents suggested below) and costume elements including the all-important red and black revolutionary hats. Throughout the play a slash / designates an overlapping of lines.

Franco's puppets can be created simply or in detail. If there is no ability to build puppets in the design, Franco can hold up paper images of the people with whom he is speaking.

Characters:
ACTOR ONE – Sasha, Sasha's Ghost
ACTOR TWO – Worker One, Ernest Hemingway (U.S.), George Orwell (English), Hermann (Cockney)
ACTOR THREE – Worker Two, Ethyl MacDonald (Scottish), Viva (Brooklyn), Virginia (Southern U.S.), Mollie (U.S.)
ACTOR FOUR – Worker Three, Dolores Iburruri (Spanish), Soledad (Spanish), Dorothy Parker (U.S.), Jason's Mum (Cockney)
ACTOR FIVE – Worker Four, Durruti (Spanish), Lorca/ Lorca's Ghost (Spanish) Conductor (Spanish), Communist Commander (Russian), Dos Passos (U.S.)

ACTOR SIX – Worker Five, Jason (Cockney), Nick (English), Waiter (Spanish), Beggar (Spanish)
ACTOR SEVEN – Emma Goldman
ACTOR EIGHT – Franco
ACTOR EIGHT uses puppets. Those puppets include: Peasant, Chamberlain, FDR, Durruti, Hitler, Stalin, etc.

> *A GUNSHOT in the dark. Three spotlights up on: 1) SASHA (ALEXANDER BERKMAN) aiming a shotgun at his own heart, 2) FRANCISCO FRANCO pointing a Gun at the audience 3) FEDERICO GARCIA LORCA in front of the firing squad.*

LORCA: Nadie está durmiendo. / En el cielo no hay, nadie durmiendo.
SASHA: No more weakness. No more cancer. / No pain.
FRANCO: God has sent me to save Spain. / From Anarchy.
LORCA: Nadie está durmiendo. Las criaturas / de la luna.
SASHA: No walking with sticks. / No weeping like a baby.
FRANCO: My Army will take Morocco. Seville will fall. / Then Barcelona.
LORCA: Las iguanas viven vendrán a morder a los hombres que no sueñan,/ y el hombre
SASHA: A sick man is no good to a revolution. / A sick man cannot defend a city.
FRANCO: Cities of Commies crushed like worms.
LORCA: Que sale corriendo con su espíritu quebrantado / se reunirán
SASHA: A sick man is nothing.
LORCA: En la esquina de la calle el caimán increíble tranquilidad. Nadie.
FRANCO: Nobody will stop me.

> *Gunshot. Blackout. In darkness we hear a phone ringing. Lights up on Emma. Emma reads what she has just written. Phone stops. She rips the paper to shreds. Mollie enters, shaken.*

MOLLIE: Emma-

EMMA: IS that Sasha? My birthday call at the final hour? He's cutting it a little close, don't you think? It's almost not even my birthday anymore.

Emma tries to get to the door. Mollie blocks her way.

EMMA: What's wrong with you?
MOLLIE: Sasha has been shot.
EMMA: What?
MOLLIE: I'm sorry, Emma.
EMMA: Who shot him?
MOLLIE: He shot himself.
EMMA: No, he didn't.
MOLLIE: I'm sorry, Emma. The cancer was too much-
EMMA: SHUT UP MOLLIE!
MOLLIE: He took a shotgun, aimed it at his heart and pulled the trigger.
EMMA: He shot himself in the heart?
MOLLIE: Then he pulled the blanket up so no one would see the blood.
EMMA: Is he dead?
MOLLIE: Not yet. He missed the heart and punctured the stomach and lungs.
EMMA: He was always a terrible shot.

Emma packs and dresses quickly.

MOLLIE: What are you doing?
EMMA: Going to France.
MOLLIE: He's bleeding badly, to get to the South of France takes a day and / a half-
EMMA: I'll be there by morning.
MOLLIE: There is nothing you can do.
EMMA: Find me a train, or an automobile.

MOLLIE: Emma-
EMMA: A TRAIN, MOLLIE!

Mollie exits.

EMMA: You shot yourself? On my birthday?

Lights out on Emma. Up on Workers.

THE WORKERS: The Insurgent Generals
WORKER ONE: Are crossing the ocean
WORKER TWO: In warships
WORKER THREE: Gathering steam
WORKER FOUR: Franco at the helm
WORKER FIVE: They are almost upon us
WORKER ONE: Speeding from Africa
THE WORKERS: Towards Spain.

Blackout. Lights up on Franco. He wheels out a trunk. Menacing grin at the audience. He wheels the trunk off. Lights up on a Bar. Three Workers and Durruti are drinking. He is gangster royalty. Wine all around.

DURRUTI: Report.
WORKER TWO: The strikers are out in full force Comrade, even in this / heat
WORKER THREE: Record breaking / heat-
WORKER ONE: Terrible heat.
DURRUTI: Are we getting water to them?
WORKER TWO: Yes, Comrade.
DURRUTI: And the People's Olympiad?
WORKER THREE: 2000 athletes have already/ arrived.
WORKER TWO: Risking their lives for sports.
DURRUTI: Not just for sports, Comrade.

WORKER THREE: Germany can host its anti-Jewish games. But everyone with a soul will come to Barcelona.
WORKER ONE: 6,000 from 22 countries. Sent by trade unions and worker's clubs.
WORKER TWO: I hope they aren't a bunch of klutzes.
WORKER THREE: Why should a communist be more of a klutz than a fascist?
WORKER ONE: You're a klutz.
WORKER THREE: I am an Anarchist.
WORKER TWO: Anarchists are good runners.
WORKER THREE: I can also swim and do the high jump.
DURRUTI: TODAY'S LESSON.
WORKER TWO: Do we have to study on such a hot day, Comrade Durruti?
WORKER THREE: Stop whining.
WORKER ONE: I don't see how Mr. Aristotle can help us.
DURRUTI: What's the first duty of a revolutionary?
ALL THREE WORKERS: Self-education.
DURRUTI: The Church has forbidden us knowledge. What is The Idea?
ALL THREE WORKERS: "To achieve a free and classless society,"
WORKER ONE: "Cooperative and intelligent,"
WORKER THREE: "Solidarity."
DURRUTI: Emma Goldman wrote: "The pupil will accept that which his mind craves." What is our common goal?
ALL THREE WORKERS: To be ready for the day the revolution begins!

He raises his glass.

DURRUTI: THE IDEA AND THE DAY!
ALL THREE WORKERS: THE IDEA AND THE DAY!

They drink. A beggar enters the bar.

BEGGAR: Senor Durruti. I am starving. Can you spare some change?

Durruti takes out a gun and points it at the Beggar. The Beggar steps back frightened. The workers freeze. A moment of tense silence, then:

DURRUTI: Take it.
BEGGAR: What?

He turns the gun around and hands it to him. The Beggar backs away.

DURRUTI: Go rob a bank.
BEGGAR: I don't understand.
DURRUTI: Why should the rich have all the money? Get some pesetas and eat.
BEGGAR: Are you joking, Senor?
DURRUTI: Bank robberies are funding the revolution.
BEGGAR: I don't want to go to prison.

Durruti stands.

DURRUTI: Walk into the bank, hold the gun like this up in the air, and say: "I DEMAND THE MONEY THAT BELONGS BY RIGHTS TO THE PEOPLE OF SPAIN!"
BEGGAR: Dios mio!
DURRUTI: Take only what you need to buy food, and after you feed yourself, feed as many others as you can. Go on.

The Beggar carefully takes the gun.

BEGGAR: I don't know how to shoot it.
DURRUTI: You don't have to shoot it. Just aim it at them. But if anyone tries to kill you, pull the trigger.

BEGGAR: You want I should bring it back after?
DURRUTI: Keep it. Fight fascism. Impress girls.
BEGGAR: Gracias, Master Durruti.
DURRUTI: Comrade Durruti. Now GO!

The Beggar runs out waving the gun.

BEGGAR: Viva la revolution.
DURRUTI: Viva la revolution.
ALL THREE WORKERS: Viva.

Lights shift. Emma races into Sasha's room, he lies in a bed barely conscious.

EMMA: Sasha.
SASHA: Emma.
EMMA: Sashenka.
SASHA: You are in England.
EMMA: I am in France. One hundred miles in six hours.
SASHA: You are fast.
EMMA: Love speeds travel, Comrade.
SASHA: You came to say goodbye.
EMMA: I came to say get better.
SASHA: It's my doing, Emma. No good to the cause. Weak old man.
EMMA: Henry Clay Frick lived 27 years after you shot him.
SASHA: 27 more minutes. Can't feel legs.
EMMA: 47 years, Sasha. Without you, I wouldn't know what to do.
SASHA: Make for me…

He coughs, trouble breathing. He closes his eyes.

EMMA: Make for you what? Open your eyes! Make what? Some soup?
SASHA: Make for me a new, free and beautiful world.
EMMA: Yes Sasha, of course.

SASHA: Spain.
EMMA: Spain?
SASHA: Listen!

> *Sasha waves his arm weakly. Lights come up on Dolores speaking to the Workers. Emma sees her.*

DOLORES: COME TO SPAIN! COMRADES THROUGHOUT THE WORLD! HEAR OUR PLEA!
THE WORKERS: VIVA !La Pasionaria!
DOLORES: FRANCO FRANQUITO IS A SHORT LITTLE PIG, A POT BELLIED TINY MAN, WITH A HIGH PITCHED DEVILISH SQUEAKY WHINE!
COME TO SPAIN! IF YOUR CITIZENSHIP IS REVOKED AS A RESULT OF COMING TO SPAIN, YOU WILL BE GRANTED CITIZENSHIP HERE. I PROMISE YOU THAT!
THE WORKERS: VIVA!
DOLORES: IT IS BETTER TO DIE ON YOUR FEET THAN LIVE ON YOUR KNEES.
THE WORKERS: BETTER TO BE THE WIDOW OF A HERO THAN THE WIFE OF A COWARD.
DOLORES: OUR BATTLE CRY HAS BEEN HEARD BY THE WHOLE WORLD
THE WORKERS: THE WORLD
DOLORES: OUR PROTESTS CANNOT BE IGNORED; WE MUST VENT OUR WRATH AND DESTROY THE ENEMY IN HIS LAIR.
DOLORES: FASCISM SHALL NOT PASS! NO PASARAN!
THE WORKERS: NO PASARAN!

> *Lights out on Dolores and The Workers.*

EMMA: She is very intense.
SASHA: You must join her.
EMMA: Sasha, I don't/ think-

SASHA: Dolores Ibárruri is known by her followers as La Pasionaria – she snuck 100 starving children into Madrid after their parents were jailed by Franco.
EMMA: Sasha/ I –
SASHA: Emma. You must go to Spain.

Sasha has a coughing fit. Franco enters rolling his trunk. Emma stares at him. He opens the trunk, takes out a puppet. He lays the puppet on the suitcase and covers it's face with a sheet and indicates that Emma do the same.

EMMA: Sasha.

She listens for his breath, kisses him and pulls the sheet over his face. She weeps. Lights out on them come up on Nick and Ethyl speaking into radio microphones on opposite sides of the stage.

NICK: Nick Reynolds with The Manchester Guardian reporting to you / from Barcelona.
ETHYL: Ethyl Macdonald from the United Socialist Movement reporting for Radio Free / Scotland.
ETHYL AND NICK: 1936.
NICK: July 18th Insurgents take /Seville.
ETHYL: July 25th Hitler agrees to Support / Franco.
NICK: The military coup by Francisco Franco, will protect British business / in the region.
ETHYL: Francisco Franco will NOT help British business, despite what the conservative press/ would have you believe.
NICK: Franco will save Europe from a Soviet takeover.
ETHYL: Franco will destroy democracy.
NICK: The savage Anarchist Beinventura Durruti leads/ the militia.
ETHYL: The revolution will abolish the oppression of the church and give the power back to / the people.
NICK: The religious and economic stability of Spain is threatened by the violent uprising of/ the workers.

ETHYL: The People's Olympiad has been cancelled. Hundreds of athletes join the workers /to defend Spain.
NICK: Liberal celebrities flock to Spain, making it their cause of the day.
ETHYL: We have the writer George Orwell on air with us today.
ORWELL: I am going to Spain to write the truth. To find out what is compelling these brave citizens to fight for freedom against Franco.
NICK: Franco's troops are in position. Each receives a double Portion of Rum. "Drink up, in the morning you will crush anarchy."
ETHYL: In the hours before dawn men, women and children take to the streets tearing up cobblestones,
NICK: Making bombs,
ETHYL: Building barricades,

Lights out on Nick and Ethyl. Lights come up on a young English man Jason at a breakfast table with his Mother. They are listening to Ethyl's voice over the radio.

ETHYL ON RADIO: Catalonian Assault Guards have executed 20,000 anarchists and pro-communist sympathizers-
JASON: Jesus Christ!
MOTHER: JASON BIDMEAD! WATCH YOUR TONGUE!
JASON: But Mum-
ETHYL ON RADIO: August 19 Federico Garcia Lorca is murdered after being forced to dig his own grave.
JASON: The killed fucking Lorca!
MOTHER: Jason! Eat your eggs.
ETHYL ON RADIO: This is a war between the Workers Republic and the Power hungry bloodthirsty Fascists.
JASON: Stupid Bloody Fascists.
ETHYL ON RADIO: This is a struggle for democracy against the forces of tyranny.
JASON: DOWN WITH THE FORCES OF TYRANNY!

Mother turns off the radio.

MOTHER: You'll be late for the Labour Exchange!
JASON: I'm goin' ta Spain!
MOTHER: Very funny.
JASON: I am.
MOTHER: You're doing no such thing, Lad. Now shut up and eat your breakfast.
JASON: I am serious, Mum.
MOTHER: Why in God's name would ya go 'ta Spain?
JASON: Because I can. Because I am on the bloody dole. Because there is a revolution on.
MOTHER: That fight's got nothing to do with you. Are you Spanish now? You never even been there on holiday.
JASON: Got to kill Franco, Mum. Save Spain.
MOTHER: Kill Franco? You couldn't kill a snail when I asked you to clear the garden!
JASON :It's for democracy Mum! To defeat the forces of tyranny.

She whacks him on the head.

MOTHER: I'll give ya the forces of tyranny, Mate. Eat your bloody eggs.

Lights shift. Emma weeps over Sasha's dead body. The sheet still covers him.

EMMA: I remember the first time we made love. I had a very narrow bed. We were squished together in the darkness. You had soft shy hands.

Lorca enters, bloodied. He stands behind her, strokes her hair.

LORCA: My Beautiful, Emma. My Little Darling…
EMMA: Sasha…I feel so drowsy.

Lorca bites her neck.

EMMA: There is an electric current rushing through me.

Lorca strokes her. She sighs.

EMMA: I would do anything for you, Alexander Berkman.
LORCA: Anything? Nada en absoluto?

Emma snaps out of her reverie and turns to look at Lorca.

EMMA :Who are you?
LORCA: Federico Garcia Lorca.
EMMA: You're bloody.
LORCA: I am dead. Buried on a hilltop in a mass grave, piled high with bodies.
EMMA: I yearn for a dead guy, and they send the wrong one.
LORCA: Sorry.
EMMA: No. You are, were, are … a very beautiful young man.
LORCA :They shot me for being on the side of those who have nothing.
EMMA: Fascists are afraid of the poor.
LORCA: They shot me for being a homosexual.
EMMA: They are terrified by their own desires.
LORCA: They shot me for subversive metaphors. Nouns that explode. They shot me because of my verbs. My verbs were the most hazardous of all.
EMMA: Your poems will live forever.
LORCA: Avenge me, Emma.
EMMA: What can I do?
LORCA: Go to Spain.

Lorca exits. Emma watches him go. Sasha grabs her hand.

EMMA: AAUUGH!

SASHA'S GHOST: Listen to the poet.
LORCA: Listen to me.
EMMA: SASHA! Are you...?
SASHA'S GHOST: Dead, Emmela. Turns out I'm not such a bad shot after all.
EMMA: OY! I'm going crazy.
LORCA: Yes, you are /nuts!
SASHA'S GHOST: I'll take it from here, Amigo.
LORCA: You want me to leave.
SASHA'S GHOST: There is a production of Bernarda Alba they are ruining in Madrid.
LORCA: I'll haunt them.

Lorca exits.

SASHA'S GHOST: You aren't going crazy, Comrade. You are walking through a land called Grief. Ghosts come with the territory.
EMMA: We don't believe in such things, Sasha.
SASHA'S GHOST: We believe in revolution, Emma. Listen to Spain!

Lights up Durruti speaking to a crowd.

DURRUTI :Come to Spain! Stop Franco! Fight against the cowardly murder of poets and dreamers! We, the workers built these cities they tear down. But we, the workers, can build others. We are not afraid of ruins. Viva la revolution!
THE WORKERS: VIVA!
EMMA: Durruti-
SASHA'S GHOST: Watch!

Franco enters with a trunk. He opens it and takes out a knife. Durruti and the Workers exit quickly. He takes out a puppet: a peasant and shouts at the puppet.

FRANCO: I am Francisco Paulino Hermenegildo Teódulo Franco. Leader of Spain, by the grace of God.

He shoots the puppet. Lights out on him. Mollie enters.

EMMA: WHAT DO YOU WANT FROM ME, SASHA?
MOLLIE: Oh, Emma. Since Sasha died you have done nothing but sit here talking to yourself.
EMMA: Not to myself.
MOLLIE: I have just gotten off the telephone with our comrades in Spain. They need you.
EMMA: What use am I them?
SASHA'S GHOST: I was attracted to you 47 years ago because of your courage.
EMMA: And all this time I thought it was my hair.
MOLLIE: What?
EMMA: I am tired.
MOLLIE: You have to find strength.
EMMA: I am not talking to you!
SASHA'S GHOST: The people need you to inspire them.
EMMA: I inspire no one.
MOLLIE: You inspire me.
EMMA: Shut up, Mollie
SASHA'S GHOST: Don't be so unkind.
EMMA: I wish I'd never loved you.
MOLLIE: Oy, Emma…
SASHA'S GHOST: Love is revolution. A true revolutionary falls madly in love with people, then does whatever it takes to save their lives. Listen to Mollie.
EMMA: OK. I'll listen to Mollie.
MOLLIE: There is a publication called SPAIN AND THE WORLD. You'd go to Barcelona to the foreign-language press office of the CNT – FAI. You'd gather information about the war and then travel back to Britain to report to the Communist Party.

EMMA: Anarchists reporting to communists? I am renown for speaking out against Stalin. British communists hate me.
SASHA'S GHOST: People have always hated us. Never stopped you before.
MOLLIE: Every anti-fascist in the world feels a thrill of hope right now because of what is happening in Spain.
SASHA'S GHOST: Emma!
EMMA: Call the comrades. I'll go to Spain.
MOLLIE: Good!

Mollie runs out. Emma glares at Sasha's Ghost. He grins. Lights shift. Nick at a microphone.

NICK: December 25th, 1936. The first Americans leave New York Harbor on the SS Normandie to fight against Franco for the Republic. British volunteers leave London by train.

An elderly British man, Hermann enters. Ethyl enters with a notebook and approaches him.

ETHYL: Excuse me sir, what is your name?
HERMANN: Hermann, Miss. Herman Feldman.
ETHYL: Where are you headed?
HERMANN: To Barcelona, Miss. To fight for the Republic.
ETHYL: Where are you from Hermann?
HERMANN: Golders Green, Miss.
ETHYL: Of Spanish heritage?
HERMANN: Polish, actually, Miss, back when.

Nick enters with note pad.

NICK: Aren't you a bit up in years for the front, Mate?
HERMANN: There are no age restrictions. Are there?
ETHYL: I am in the middle of an interview here.
NICK: Have you ever fired a gun, Old Boy?

HERMANN: They are going to teach me. Aren't they?

NICK: The left has an army of aging inexperienced jellyfish, while Franco's militia is young, fit and ready for battle.

ETHYL: Why don't you piss off?

NICK: Sir, why are you going to fight a Civil War in a foreign country that has nothing to do with you?

HERMANN: The Rabbi tells us we must do the right thing. Stand up for the downtrodden.

NICK: Rabbi going to fight in Spain, is he?

ETHYL: Go away.

NICK: Gladly. Ernest Hemingway and Dorothy Parker are getting off a ship from the U.S. I'll interview the big American fish; you stick with the Cockney tadpoles.

Nick exits. Lorca and Sasha enter.

HERMANN: The Rabbi isn't coming Miss, but my whole mob from the pub has gone. Have you seen a bloke by the name of George Montague? He's a pipe – smoking fellow with clipped moustache. From Bethnal Green?

ETHYL: No, sorry I haven't –

LORCA: Major Montague. Killed in action at Torra le Donas-

HERMANN: Morris Manfred Lazar, Belsize Park?

SASHA'S GHOST: Made it through the Spanish war but was murdered in Stalin's purges of 1954.

HERMANN: Harry Groeser? His father owns a small sweet shop in Highgate. Harry was in the Jewish Lads Brigade. When his family found out he was going to Spain they hid his clothes. But he went anyway.

LORCA: Shot dead in Madrid.

ETHYL: I haven't met any of your friends yet, Hermann. How do you feel about going to the front?

HERMANN: Fighting Franco is the right thing to do. Isn't it?

ETHYL: Of course it is, Hermann.

SASHA'S GHOST: Lt. Herman L. Feldman – acting commander No 2 Group. Killed in action on the Aragon front.
LORCA: Two years later 12 of his Polish relatives are murdered in Auschwitz.
ETHYL: Good Luck, Soldier.
HERMANN: Ta, Miss.
SASHA'S GHOST: All these good women and all these good men.
LORCA: Which ones will be ghosts before this war's end?
SASHA'S GHOST: Who dies by the gun, who by the knife?
LORCA: Who loses his son, who mourns his poor wife?
SASHA'S GHOST: I will swim in the blood.
LORCA: I will befriend all the dead.
SASHA'S GHOST: But not Goldman.
LORCA: Not yet.

He exits. Lights shift. The port. Nick approaches Ernest Hemingway who is exiting a ship.

NICK: Ernest Hemingway! Nick Reynolds, Manchester Guardian. How do you feel about going back to Spain?
HEMINGWAY: Love Spain. Love the food. Love the women. Love the bulls. I'm going to get a great book out of this revolution.

Dorothy Parker, and Virginia enter behind him.

NICK: Miss Dorothy Parker. You are from the New Yorker magazine to write about the war in Spain?
DOROTHY PARKER: Unlike Hemingway, I am not going to spend time in some bullring. Though I do enjoy a bullfighter from time to time. I will steep myself in the true lives at the front lines.
HEMINGWAY: All the American and European liberals are in a sweaty race to see who can get shot first.
VIRGINIA: Not me.

DOROTHY PARKER: No Darling. No one would ever accuse you of sweating.
NICK: Who are you?
HEMINGWAY: A pretty friend.
NICK: And why are you going to Spain, Pretty Friend?
VIRGINIA: Hem says it's the most exciting spot in Europe these days.
HEMINGWAY: That's off the record, Buddy.
VIRGINIA: I might write a little book of my own.
DOROTHY PARKER: Yes, a very little book. But do be careful, Duckie. War zones tend to give you runs in your stockings.
VIRGINIA: I don't like her, Hem.
DOROTHY PARKER: That's OK, Sweetie. Hardly anyone does.

Dos Passos enters.

DOS PASSOS: We had better get to the train. There's a huge crowd gathering. Dot do you have the tickets?
DOROTHY: Come along, Princess. Let's get some decent seats.

Dorothy exits pulling Virginia after her.

NICK: Mr. Dos Passos, you are making a film about the revolution in Spain?
DOS PASSOS: The Spanish Earth.
NICK: Propaganda?
DOS PASSOS: Art.
HEMINGWAY: Horseshit.
DOS PASSOS: Viva L'Espana!
HEMINGWAY: Yeah, yeah, viva, viva…

He pulls Dos Passos off. Lights shift. Spain. Soledad is folding laundry with a rifle over one shoulder. Ethyl enters with a note pad.

ETHYL: Are you Soledad Serrantos the leader of Mujeres Libres?
SOLEDAD: Who wants to know?

ETHYL: Ethyl MacDonald, Radio Free Barcelona.
SOLEDAD: Anarchist?

Ethyl nods. Soledad offers her hand.

ETHYL: Why are you folding laundry in the middle of the revolution?
SOLEDAD: My husband needs clean underwear.
ETHYL: Emma Goldman wrote: "Women need internal emancipation to know their own value, respect themselves, and refuse to be slaves to male lovers."
SOLEDAD: She also wrote: "Before we can forgive one another, we have to understand one another." Spain is a different world for you Sister.
ETHYL: I just got here.
SOLEDAD: When we defeat fascism it will have nothing to do with who washes my husband's underpants.
ETHYL: Aren't you a feminist?
SOLEDAD: In my country the word Feminista means upper class women who call for bourgeois political reform. We are working class women trying to make life better for our families.
ETHYL: So what are you doing with that gun?
SOLEDAD: I am a militia fighter with the Durruti column. Tomorrow I leave for the front. Today I fold my husband's underwear. Embrace the dialectic.
ETHYL: How does your husband feel about you leaving for the front?
SOLEDAD: The only important thing is to save Spain. The Republic is more important than family, more important than comfort, than love. He will do his part. My three boys will do their parts. And I will do mine.
ETHYL: With Durruti.
SOLEDAD: I am lucky to serve under my hero.

Nick enters, note pad in hand.

NICK: Are you Mujeres Libres? The girl's group threatening to overthrow Franco's army with spoons and spatulas?
SOLEDAD: Who are you?
ETHYL: Nick Reynolds, Manchester Guardian. I recognized the strident voice from his fascist radio show.
NICK: You must be Ethyl Burn-It-All-Down Mac Donald.

Soledad points the gun at his chest.

SOLEDAD: Be polite to her.
NICK: I predict you'll shoot yourself in the foot with that pistol within a week.

Soledad pokes his chest with the gun.

SOLEDAD: It's a rifle. Get away from us.

Nick exits. Soledad shouts after him.

SOLEDAD: Viva L'Espana!
ETHYL: Viva!

Ethyl picks up some laundry and helps Soledad fold. Lights shift. Franco enters with a suitcase. He opens it, takes out a puppet. He shouts at it.

FRANCO: I, Francisco Franco, will save Spain as a Christian nation of purity and Godliness and wealth. I will prevail over the forces of chaos and the free reign of anarchist evil!

He takes out a noose. He hangs the puppet. He marches off stage swinging the dead puppet. Lights shift.

A train. Jason and Hermann are sitting near each other. Emma is sitting further away. Viva sits with a small suitcase. She looks out the window of the train. Hermann is nervously tapping his feet. Jason and Emma are writing letters. Suddenly Hermann jumps to his feet. Emma and Viva look up.

HERMANN: I don't want to go. It's not my battle. I don't want to die. I want to go home. Let me off this train!
JASON: Get off then, old fool. You are chicken! Not the sort of bloke we want in Spain!

A conductor comes by.

CONDUCTOR: Boletos, por favor, de que los boletos!
JASON: How much?
CONDUCTOR: You come to fight?
JASON: Yes.
CONDUCTOR: Which side?
JASON: We're here with the International Brigades, to fight / Franco.
HERMANN: Quiet Mate, you don't know what side he's on.

The Conductor looks at Viva.

CONDUCTOR: Boletos!
VIVA: Do you speak-?
CONDUCTOR: English? Small.
VIVA: My passport is stamped: Not For Use In Spain.
EMMA: Careful, young lady.
VIVA: They told me some of the train conductors are with us.
CONDUCTOR: With who?
VIVA: The Abraham Lincoln Brigade. I am a nurse.
CONDUCTOR: Could be danger for you here.
VIVA: I just finished my nursing certificate at Brooklyn College. I'm not afraid of anything.

He walks over to Emma.

CONDUCTOR: You are-?
EMMA: Emma Goldman.
CONDUCTOR: Your picture I see before.
EMMA: Ah.
CONDUCTOR: Confession!
EMMA: Confession?
CONDUCTOR: I am a good Catholic. My family are Nationalists. We are strong behind Franco to save Spain from poverty and sin.
HERMANN: Oh Dear.
EMMA: You are CEDA?
VIVA: What is CEDA?

Emma keeps her eyes on the Conductor.

EMMA: The CEDA is a Catholic right-wing political organization dedicated to anti-Marxism which claims that it is defending Spain and "Christian civilization" from the deviants.
CONDUCTOR: A man in the street he gave me your book.
EMMA: Yes?
CONDUCTOR: That was the beginning of my fury.
EMMA: And what are you doing with your fury?
CONDUCTOR: I go to fight with Durruti.
EMMA: Good for you, Comrade.

She shakes his hand. Everyone breathes a sigh of relief. The Conductor throws his arms around Jason.

CONDUCTOR: No pay. You ride free. He with you?

The Conductor points at Hermann.

HERMANN: Yes. Yes, I am with him.

He sits back down in his seat.

ONDUCTOR: Welcome to Spain, All of you. Welcome to Spain.

The train stops.

CONDUCTOR: Barcelona!

Lights shift. MUSIC.

EMMA: Barcelona!

Emma stands with her suitcase center stage. People surround her. Some carry grain, some carry machine parts. Busy in their work they don't hear her.

EMMA: Hello, Comrades. I am…Emma Goldman….I am here to report your efforts to the English speaking world… Hello. What the am I doing here?…Uh…Hello? Viva la Revolution!
THE WORKERS: VIVA!
EMMA: Viva L'Espana!
THE WORKERS: VIVA! VIVA! VIVA!
EMMA: I see the work you are doing, here.
THE WORKERS: The work!
WORKER TWO: Building a new world
EMMA: A new and beautiful world.
THE WORKERS: VIVA justice! VIVA freedom! VIVA revolution!
EMMA: Oh Sasha, they are filled with such spirit.
THE WORKERS: JOIN US!
EMMA: Like you and I when we were young.
WORKER ONE: Look around you!
WORKER TWO The revolution
WORKER THREE: You dreamed about
WORKER FOUR: Is happening!
EMMA: What a foaming sea of life is
THE WORKERS: Barcelona.
EMMA: The streets are thronging.

THE WORKERS: With work! With song.
WORKER FIVE: The people are
WORKER ONE: Shouting from rooftops.
WORKER FIVE: Busy with the labors of survival.
WORKER TWO: Revival.
THE WORKERS: Life!
WORKER THREE: Shelter.
WORKER FOUR: Clean Water.
WORKER FIVE: The means of Defense.
EMMA: Sasha, everything makes sense.
THE WORKERS: VIVA!
WORKER ONE: People in the streets.
WORKER TWO: The mighty feat
WORKER THREE: Of holding firm
WORKER FOUR: To Barcelona.
WORKER FIVE: Viva!
THE WORKERS: VIVA!
WORKER ONE: Six hours after the coup
WORKER TWO: The city is working again.
WORKER THREE: Trams and trade unions
WORKER FOUR: Cinemas and food supplies
WORKER FIVE: A functional economy
WORKER ONE: Our shining city
WORKER TWO: No pity!
WORKER THREE: For the enemy fakes!
WORKER FOUR: Franco's snakes!
WORKER FIVE: We stand up to face
THE WORKERS: The Church.
WORKER ONE: No more grief,
WORKER TWO: From priests,
WORKER THREE: Telling us how to live and what to think
WORKER FOUR: And what to say and not to drink
THE WORKERS: Destroy the Cathedrals! Tear the statues down!
WORKER FIVE: Drag the Crosses and the Mummies to the streets
WORKER THREE: Rip the Pope's prisons down

WORKER FOUR: Burn them to the ground
WORKER FIVE: But save the Gaudi one.
WORKER ONE: Because he wasn't done.
EMMA: Such is the logic of Revolution
THE WORKERS: WATCH OUT!
WORKER TWO: Stand strong!
THE WORKERS: Here come the war planes and bombs.
EMMA: Such courage!
WORKER THREE: No longer oppressed by the upper classes
WORKER FOUR: The masses
WORKER FIVE: Strive.
WORER ONE: To stay alive.
THE WORKERS: Hunger. Blood.
WORKER TWO: The flood of people pouring into
THE WORKERS: Barcelona
WORKER THREE: Granada, Madrid, Valencia
WORKER FOUR: From England, Mexico, Russia
EMMA: The International Brigades!
WORKER FIVE: Making waves.
THE WORKERS: FOR SPAIN.
WORKER ONE: For a new life.
WORKER TWO: To believe! To dare!
WORKER THREE: Everything is shared!
THE WORKERS: VIVA
WORKER FOUR: A hungry man on the street is handed bread by two passersby.
WORKER FIVE: Without begging, a woman and her baby are fed by strangers.
THE WORKERS: Comrades. Sisters. Mothers. Lovers. Brothers
WORKER ONE: Unite.
WORKER TWO: In the fight
WORKER ONE: For freedom
THE WORKERS: VIVA
WORKER THREE: Neighbors bring blankets for neighbors.
WORKER FOUR: We keep watch at night.

WORKER FIVE: Whisper passwords. Flick the blue code light.
WORKER ONE: We organize. We plan.
WORKER TWO :Man to Woman.
WORKER THREE: Woman to Man.
THE WORKERS: VIVA!
EMMA: VIVA!
WORKER FOUR: All the farms of Spain are now collectives.
WORKER FIVE: No longer selective, the houses and factories belonging to the rich
WORKER ONE: Are requisitioned.
WORKER TWO: And cars!
THE WORKERS: CARS!
WORKER THREE: We've never had cars.
WORKER FOUR: We take the cars of bourgeoisie
WORKER FIVE: Their Rolls Royce's, their Mercedes
WORKER ONE: Even though we don't know how
WORKER TWO: To drive
WORKER THREE: We do it fast.
WORKER FOUR: Sometimes
THE WORKERS: We crash.
WORKER ONE: The fancy restaurant at The Ritz Hotel.
WORKER TWO: Is reclaimed and renamed
THE WORKERS: Gastronomie Unit Number One
WORKER THREE: Now everyone eats there.
WORKER ONE: No Hats!
WORKER TWO: Only the red and the black
WORKER THREE: All other hats are for the bourgeoisie
WORKER FOUR: Not for you
EMMA: Not for me

Emma takes off her hat.

THE WORKERS: VIVA
EMMA: VIVA

THE WORKERS: Long live Spain!
EMMA: SPAIN!
THE WORKERS: 16,000 people gather
WORKER ONE: To hear Emma Goldman
WORKER TWO: Comrade Durruti
WORKER FIVE: And La Pasionara
WORKER FOUR: Speak
THE WORKERS: To Barcelona!
WORKER FOUR: VIVA!
WORKER FIVE: VIVA!
EMMA: VIVA!
THE WORKERS: VIVA! VIVA! VIVA!
EMMA: COMRADES OF SPAIN. YOU AMAZE ME. LOOK AT THESE CROWDS! YOUR
IDEALS ARE MY IDEALS! MY ONE DESIRE NOW IS TO BE A PART,
GREAT OR SMALL OF THE BATTLE YOU ARE MAKING. CATALONIA IS THE FREEST PLACE IN THE WORLD. VIVA!
THE WORKERS: VIVA!

Dolores ENTERS. Sasha's Ghost and Lorca appear.

EMMA: La Pasionaria.
DOLORES: Emma Goldman. Bienvenido a España.
EMMA: It is an honor to meet such a vibrant force of the revolution.
DOLORES: A "vibrant force" of the Communist party.
EMMA: Our struggle is the same.
DOLORES: You speak publicly against Comrade Stalin.
EMMA: Comrade Stalin is a murderer.
DOLORES: Comrade Stalin is the only hope for Spain. The English and the Americans will turn away from us. Franco has Germany and Italy. Russia is our friend.
EMMA: When I go back and inform the British of the great work happening here, the left will galvanize the world.

DOLORES: You are naïve, Comrade. If I were you I would think about writing a formal apology to the Supreme Soviet of the Union of Soviet Socialist Republics. You are good with words.
EMMA: An apology.
LORCA: Oh Dear. I am too squeamish to watch the battle of the revolutionist divas.

Lorca leaves.

SASHA'S GHOST: Emma, don't fight with this one. Please. Breathe.

Emma takes a deep breath.

EMMA: Let's not unleash our differences at this vital moment of history.
DOLORES: At some point the revolution may force us to do so.
EMMA: At some point La Pasionara, but not on this magnificent day.
DOLORES: Be careful, Goldman. Spain can be hazardous to your health.

Dolores exits.

SASHA'S GHOST: Your handsome young warrior approaches.

Sasha exits. Durruti approaches Emma and bows.

EMMA: Durruti!
DURRUTI: I had to come greet you myself, Comrade Goldman. Your writings have inspired me since I was a young boy.
EMMA: A young boy. Imagine that. I've heard such wonderful stories about your work. You are proving to the world that Anarchism is worth fighting for.
DURRUTI: Would you like to come see our operation at the front?
EMMA: I would love it!

DURRUTI: I must warn you of the danger. Especially-
EMMA: For an old woman?
DURRUTI: Spain is perilous.
EMMA: And glorious.
DURRUTI: See you at the front.
EMMA: Viva!

He bows and exits.

EMMA: What a good-looking young man.

George Orwell enters.

GEORGE ORWELL: Emma Goldman! George Orwell.
EMMA: I have read your excellent portrait of the working poor in Northern England.
GEORGE ORWELL: Thank you.
EMMA: You've come here like Hemingway to write about the war?
GEORGE ORWELL: I came here to write as unlike Hemingway as humanly possible. I am taken over by the spirit of the people.
EMMA: So am I!
GEORGE ORWELL: The vigor and the enthusiasm!
EMMA: The bravery and the hope!
GEORGE ORWELL: Do you realize there are no fancily dressed people on the streets at all? No hats except the red and black. It is truly a workers state! I am headed to the front.
EMMA: You came to write, and you stay to fight.
GEORGE ORWELL: It seems the only conceivable thing to do.
EMMA: If I was younger I'd do the same. Good luck to you.
ORWELL: And to you.

They shake hands. He exits. Ethyl enters.

ETHYL: Emma Goldman. Ethyl MacDonald. I can't tell you how honored I am to meet you.

EMMA: We've all enjoyed your nightly broadcasts, not only because of your excellent reportage, but because you have one of the finest radio voices we have ever heard.

ETHYL: I try to make up for my bad Spanish with slightly better English. But the revolution is much better off now because you are here. But your voice is much stronger than mine.

EMMA: I just hope that I can be useful to Spain. Tell me everything.

ETHYL: The workers have turned the movie houses into communal dining halls. But we show Charlie Chaplain films to keep morale up.

EMMA: Do you have enough to eat?

ETHYL: We go around to shops and requisition bread. The shopkeepers aren't exactly happy about it-but they do it because it is necessary for the revolution.

EMMA: Our comrades are not just fighting a common enemy they are building a dream!

Nick enters with a note pad.

NICK: "The Most Dangerous Woman in America."

EMMA: Who are you?

NICK: Nick Reynolds. Manchester Guardian. Aren't you frightened to be wandering through a civil war, Grandma Anarchy?

ETHYL: He's a conservative pundit of right wing yellow journalism.

EMMA: I warn you, young fellow, if you write the war badly you'll end the war badly. You will be just as much our enemy as Franco. Be careful. Grandma Anarchy will hunt you down and break your writing hand.

Nick laughs and exits.

ETHYL: I must do my broadcast, Emma. Today it will be all about you coming to Spain! VIVA!

EMMA: VIVA!

Ethyl runs off.

EMMA: So many lovely people here, Sasha. I may have to fall in love again just one more time.

Lights shift. Hotel Florida. Hemingway eats a big plate of bacon and eggs. Dos Passos and Dorothy sit across from him. Jason and Viva sit on the opposite side of the room staring at Hemingway's plate of food.

DOS PASSOS: You know that people are starving in Spain.
HEMINGWAY: There is a war on! Starvation is part of the ambiance.
DOROTHY PARKER: You are permeating the room with the aroma of bacon. Frankly it's cruel, Hem.
HEMINGWAY: I offered you some Dot.
DOS PASSOS: Yes and she is using all of her will power to refuse.
HEMINGWAY: Why?
DOS PASSOS: Because she has a heart in her, man. There is a soldier with his girl over there looking close to fainting from hunger.
HEMINGWAY: You want me to feed everyone in Spain?
DOROTHY PARKER: No, but you don't have to flaunt the meat you smuggled from your bullfighting boys while the rest of the country is famished.
HEMINGWAY: HEY SOLDIER!
JASON: Yes Sir?
HEMINGWAY: Where are you from?
JASON: England, Sir.
HEMINGWAY: Cockney Express?
JASON: I guess so, Sir.
HEMINGWAY: And your girlfriend?
VIVA: I don't even know him. I'm just sitting here.
HEMINGWAY: Where are you from?
VIVA: Brooklyn.
HEMINGWAY: Are you hungry, Brooklyn?

VIVA: I'm OK.
DOROTHY PARKER: When is the last time you ate, dear?
VIVA: Yesterday.
DOS PASSOS: What about you soldier?
JASON: I'm fine, Sir.
HEMINGWAY: Oh for God's sakes. Come finish my plate! Come on Skinny
Brooklyn!
VIVA: No, thank you.
HEMINGWAY: Cockney Express!
JASON: I don't want to take your last bite.
DOROTHY PARKER: Believe me, it's not his last bite. He's got a stash upstairs in his room that would shame a Parisian bistro.
HEMINGWAY: You are a pain in my ass, Dot.
DOS PASSOS: What are you even doing in Spain?
HEMINGWAY: I am writing an important novel that will be read by every American for centuries to come.
DOS PASSOS: God help the centuries to come.
HEMINGWAY: You consider writing some kind of duty. It's not a passion with you. You're not a…
DOS PASSOS: I'm not a what? A Hemingway?
DOROTHY PARKER: OK Boys. I'm going to see the real war.

Dorothy exits. Dos Passos exits. Hemingway lurches after them. Jason leans towards Viva.

JASON: That was Ernest Hemingway. The writer.
VIVA: Did he really expect us to eat off his plate?
JASON: I dunno. But I wish I had.
VIVA: So do I.
JASON: You feeling weak?
VIVA: I'm not complaining!
JASON: I never said you were.
VIVA: What's the Cockney Express?

JASON: It's all of us working class geezers with nowhere else to be but The Aragon Front.
VIVA: Is that where you're headed?
JASON: Durruti column.
VIVA: Me too. That's great!

Pause.

JASON: You're not scared?
VIVA: Why should I be scared? Because I'm a girl?
JASON: No! I mean… No. But sometimes…
VIVA: Sometimes what?
JASON: Well sometimes… I mean… I've never shot a gun nor killed… well, anything, not even a snail….
VIVA: When I was a kid, my mother told me about this fire that broke out in a movie house in Chicago. Everybody panicked. Women and children were trampled on by big men racing to the doors. I always worried about that – about what I'd do in a well, an emergency. I hope I'll behave nobly. I mean, I hope I don't…
JASON: Duck?
VIVA: Exactly.
JASON: What's your name?
VIVA: Viva.
JASON: Like Viva la Revolution?
VIVA: I changed my name on the boat.
JASON: Really?
VIVA: Midway between Paris and Pembroke I threw my library card off the side of the ship. Bye – bye Viv Weinblatt. Hello Viva. Do you think my Mother will ever forgive me?
JASON: How does she feel about you being here?
VIVA: She took her precious Star Of David from her neck and put it on mine. She said "don't take it off no matter what. It will save your life." What about you?
JASON: My mother didn't give me a necklace.

VIVA: No. Your Name.
JASON: Oh. Jason.
VIVA: Maybe we should go find something to eat, Jason.
JASON: There's got to be a stale biscuit around here somewhere.
VIVA: Come on.

> *She pulls him off stage. Lights shift. THE FRONT. Emma staggers into Durutti's headquarters after a grueling trek. It's evening. Durruti is with soldiers (Hermann, Viva and Jason) busily cleaning and re-building old rifles.*

DURRUTI: Comrade, Goldman! You made it!
EMMA: I hope I will not be in the way.
DURRUTI: We are preparing for a big incursion in the morning. Can you build a Molotov cocktail?
EMMA: I'm a little rusty. In the near distance there is shelling.
DURRUTI: Can I get you something to eat? We don't have much, but I can find something.
EMMA: Please don't worry about me, go on with your work.
DURRUTI: At daybreak we will try to drive the enemy back, and hopefully we will succeed in capturing arms – we have 10,000 volunteers and only 3,000 working guns.

> *Soledad enters.*

SOLEDAD: Comrade Durruti, we've almost finished the first load of guns. We'll start on the second crate after training.
DURRUTI: We should push through now, don't you think? Easier to build guns in daylight.
SOLEDAD: Hands are getting tired.
DURRUTI: Whatever you think is best.
EMMA: Can I do something to help?
SOLEDAD: Do you know how to break down a Mauser pistol? Or a bolt action rifle? I have a model from 1895 that is missing some parts.
EMMA: Sorry.

SOLEDAD: That's OK, I'll get Durruti to do it. He's lousy with the newer guns, but he can make the ancient junk work like magic.
EMMA: Your commander works alongside you.
SOLEDAD: Of course. Every task is shared equally.
EMMA: But you respect him very much.
SOLEDAD: He never plays the part of a superior. He's one of us. Eats and sleeps as we do. Denies himself his own portion of food if one of us is weak or sick.
EMMA: What can I do to help you?
SOLEDAD: Do you have a lipstick?
EMMA: A lipstick?
SOLEDAD: Mine was lost weeks ago. I'd like one for the trench.

Emma digs around in her bag, finds one, hands it to Soledad.

EMMA: I use this to moisten my lips for public speaking. It's bright red. But if you don't mind my asking-?
SOLEDAD: When the Nationalists shoot me, I want them to know they are killing a beautiful woman. Excuse me, Comrade.

Soledad joins the other soldiers building guns.

EMMA: How have you succeeded in welding together a band of thousands of motley volunteers who follow you of their own volition?
DURRUTI: I am surprised that you, a seasoned lifelong anarchist, and my great hero, should ask me such a question. Haven't you inspired the masses for over forty years?
EMMA: I have never gotten thousands of men and women to risk their lives in the face of enemy fire.
DURRUTI: These people have come to me. Ready to stake their lives in our fight. I consider discipline indispensable, but it must be inner discipline, motivated by comradeship.
EMMA: Listening to you, I am tempted to throw my old body at the enemy to block even one bullet.

DURRUTI: Your presence here is uplifting for us, Comrade. You don't need to throw yourself at anything.

Hermann approaches Durruti.

HERMANN: Can I speak with you, Comrade Durruti?
DURRUTI: Of course.
HERMANN: I need to take a leave from the front.
DURRUTI: We are moving into the trenches at dawn.
HERMANN: I have to leave tonight.
DURRUTI: Why, Hermann?
HERMANN: My family back in London is very poor. I just got word that my sister is failing. I need to go help her.
DURRUTI: So you want to leave the fighting line just before the incursion?
HERMANN: I should go now.
DURRUTI: That is fine, Hermann. You do understand that we are fighting because your family and so many like them are living under conditions of poverty, don't you?
HERMANN: Yes. But-
DURRUTI: By our victory everyone will be able to live decently. Your sister and everyone else's sister. That fellow over there has a small son living in a dirt floor shack. That one has a six month old baby girl. Go over there now and tell those comrades that they will have one less able body at the front in the morning.
HERMANN: I can't do that.
DURRUTI: Don't you see Hermann, the revolution you and I are waging will safeguard the poor and do away with the suffering of people like your sister. You are an essential part of our struggle. Do you see that, Comrade?
HERMANN: Please, Comrade Durruti, forgive me for asking. Forget I mentioned it. Please let me stay.
DURRUTI: Of course you can stay, Comrade.
HERMANN: Thank you. Thank you Comrade, Durruti.

Hermann goes back to work.

EMMA: If I were thirty, well... even twenty... ten years younger...
DURRUTI: What would you do?
EMMA: I would pull you into the nearest haystack and show you how you've ignited passion in me that I thought was long deceased.
DURRUTI: You will be passionate until your last breath Emma. And if I didn't have to launch an attack at daybreak...
EMMA: Don't tease an old woman.

Jason and Viva approach.

JASON: Comrade.
DURRUTI: Yes, Jason.
JASON: Maybe Viva should stay here tomorrow, Sir. Care for the wounded as they come back from the trenches.
VIVA: You've got to be kidding.
JASON: I just think with the rate of casualties, we should have a nurse at headquarters.
VIVA: I am going to the trenches just like you.
JASON: I am trying to be a gentleman.
VIVA: Do not be a gentleman.

She drags him back to the guns.

EMMA: You have many casualties?
DURRUTI: Most are self-inflicted. Our soldiers are kids, farmers, factory workers, who have never handled a gun, much less fired one. We have few supplies. We clean guns with olive oil or bacon fat. There are no lanterns, no electric torches, no maps, no charts. But my troops are undaunted. RIGHT, COMRADES?
SOLEDAD, VIVA, JASON AND HERMANN: We stand and fall with Durruti!

Lights shift. Franco with his suitcase. He opens it, takes out a puppet. He takes a sharp knife and begins torturing the puppet with the blade, holds it to the puppet's throat.

FRANCO: SPEAK, PIG! WHERE IS DURRUTI'S CAMP? WHERE IS THE LITTLE ANARCHIST SHIT? SPEAK! YOU UGLY COMMUNIST PIG! SPEAK!

Lights out on Franco and up on Durruti. It's midnight and he is alone looking over some maps. Soledad enters, wearing red lipstick.

SOLEDAD: Is there anything you need, Comrade Durruti?
DURRUTI: Are the guns built?
SOLEDAD: Yes, Comrade.
DURRUTI: The troops fed?
SOLEDAD: Yes, Comrade.
DURRUTI: Are they ready?
SOLEDAD: As ready as possible. They are sleeping.
DURRUTI: Then you've done everything beautifully, Soledad. Tomorrow you will lead the action in the second trench from enemy lines. I'll be in the first.
SOLEDAD: Do you ever get scared, Comrade?
DURRUTI: I never stop being scared, Comrade.
SOLEDAD: You never show it.
DURRUTI: You don't see it in my eyes?
SOLEDAD: No.
DURRUTI: You don't hear it in my voice?

He kisses her.

DURRUTI: Can you taste it?
SOLEDAD: A little.
DURRUTI: Your lips are blood red.

He kisses her again.

SOLEDAD: I love you.
DURRUTI: You love Spain. I am just a vessel for your patriotism.
SOLEDAD: I'd like to spend the night with my patriotism. It could be my last night on earth.
DURRUTI: You have a husband.
SOLEDAD: He is in some trench waiting for the morning's first gunshots. I hope he is in someone's arms tonight.

Durruti leads her off.

Lights shift. The next morning. The trenches. Heavy shelling. Jason, Viva, Soledad, The Conductor, and Hermann are hunkered down. Everyone but Viva fires repeatedly from the trench. Viva folds and organizes bandages. Shelling dies down.
SOLEDAD: There is a woman in the village about to give birth.
VIVA: We should try to get to her.
JASON: No. It means crossing open land with no cover. Stay in the trench.
VIVA: There are no medical supplies in the village.
SOLIDAD: Her husband is in the next trench – he begged me.
JASON: Too dangerous.
SOLEDAD: Danger is everywhere. We spent an hour arguing last night about whether to sleep with our boots on because the extra 17 seconds to pull them on could be a matter of life and death.
VIVA: If a nurse can't save a woman and her baby, what good is she?
JASON: Stay put.
VIVA: Stop protecting me.
JASON: Soledad, how does your husband feel about you being in a trench?
SOLEDAD: His parents were some of Franco's first casualties. It is the right and duty of every Spaniard to fight. There is nothing more important than this. Follow Durruti. Save Spain.

HERMAN: I am hungry.
CONDUCTOR: You are always hungry.
HERMANN: When does food come, Senorita?
VIVA: Why are you asking me? Do I look like a waitress?
Shelling very close. Soledad drops to the ground and fires back. Hermann fires his gun and it backfires sending him to the ground. Jason goes to him.
JASON: You alright, Mate?
HERMANN: Old gun.
CONDUCTOR: This is not a war it's a comedy.
HERMANN: Is there any more bread?
CONDUCTOR: No.
HERMANN: You ate the last bit of bread!
CONDUCTOR: Something smells bad.
HERMANN: It's you.
SOLEDAD: We are out of firewood, tobacco, candles, matches and bread. Someone has to get supplies.
JASON: It's Hermann's turn to go.
HERMANN: Mine?
JASON: You've got to go to the post. Just past the sentry.
SOLEDAD: Be careful. Between there and here is a hundred yards of flat ground with hardly enough cover for a rabbit.
HERMANN: It's too dangerous. I won't go.
JASON: Yes you will, mate. It's your turn.
HERMANN: No!

Jason knocks him down.

JASON: I'll bloody drag you there myself.
HERMANN: HELP!
CONDUCTOR: Leave him alone, Fascist!

The Conductor grabs Jason.

VIVA: Let go of him!

CONDUCTOR: I am a good Catholic. I shouldn't be out here with whores!
JASON: Shut up!
CONDUCTOR: You shut up!
SOLEDAD: STOP IT! You're acting like children!
JASON: She's right.

He picks Hermann up.

CONDUCTOR: Sorry.
VIVA: Sorry.
CONDUCTOR: I did not mean to call you a whore. I'm just hungry.
HERMANN: I'll get the supplies.
JASON: You know how to get through the checkpoint, right?
HERMANN: Uh … I say the password
SOLEDAD: Don't forget to say the right one.
HERMANN: Hold on. It's something about Granada …
JASON: That was yesterday's. We got the new one this morning.
HERMANN: I don't remember!
JASON: The password today is Cataluna – Eroica.
HERMANN: I say Cataluna – Eroica?
JASON: No the sentry says Cataluna, and you answer Eroica
HERMANN: I don't even know what Eroica means
JASON: I think it's the like Valiente.
SOLEDAD: Eroica is similar to Valiente.
CONDUCTOR: Means pretty much the same thing.
HERMANN: Valiente?
SOLEDAD: Eroica.
JASON: You ready?
HERMANN: Think so.
SOLEDAD: Don't forget your gun.
HERMANN: OK. Here I go.
JASON: Good luck.

Hermann exits.

THE SENTRY (OFF STAGE): CATALANA!
HERMANN (OFF STAGE): VALIENTE!
JASON: SHIT!

A shot. And a scream offstage.

HERMANN (OFF STAGE): You shot me in the bloody leg! I'm on your side!

Viva gathers her bag. Gunfire from offstage. Jason throws his arms over Viva.

JASON: Here we are, soldiers of a revolutionary army.
VIVA: Defending Democracy against Fascism.
JASON: Defeating the forces of tyranny.
VIVA: Heroes.
JASON: So why does it feel like we're in a Charlie Chaplain movie?

He pulls her towards him and kisses her. Lights shift.
Franco enters stabbing the puppet he is holding. Nick enters.

NICK: General Franco. Nick Reynolds, Manchester Guardian. Can you answer some questions?

Franco puts the puppet back in the case.

FRANCO: Are you the press that loves me or the press that hates me?
NICK: The British government has quietly supported your efforts to stop the force of Soviet communism from taking over the world. I am a loyal British citizen.
FRANCO: What are your questions?
NICK: Tell us your chances for victory.
FRANCO: I will be victorious.
NICK: What will it take for you to win Spain?

FRANCO: I will pay any price for victory
NICK: Even if you have to kill half the country?
FRANCO: Any price.
NICK: Hitler and Mussolini are solidly behind you. What do you think England and America will do?

Franco takes two puppets out of his trunk: Chamberlain and FDR.

FRANCO: Hello Mr. Chamberlain. Hello Mr. President
Hitler and Mussolini are solidly for me. What are you two fools going to do?
(as FDR)
Are you going to help the Republic, Mr. Chamberlain?
(as Chamberlain)
I will do what is good for England, Mr. President. Britain has many business interests in Spain. What are you going to do?
(as FDR)
I will do what is best for the United States. Franco has the backing and the money. I am no fan of Hitler of course, But well… this is a quandary. We have to keep our people safe.
(as Chamberlain)
My Spanish Ambassador is in a quite nice hotel on the French side. Keeping him out of Spain all together.
(as FDR)
Mine too. Just over the border. Biarritz.
(as Chamberlain)
Lovely cheese in Biarritz.
(as FDR)
Spain is a vicarious sacrifice.
(as Chamberlain)
We should stay out of the whole mess. See what the rest of the world decides to do.
FRANCO (as FDR):We'll need to make some sort of statement, I suppose.
(as Chamberlain)

NON INTERVENTION.

He puts the puppets back in the suitcase.

NICK: Non-Intervention.
FRANCO: The western rulers without balls wait around for their friends to decide. Meanwhile Hitler and Mussolini have los testículos I need.
NICK: To win.
FRANCO: Of course to win.. Write that in your newspaper. Write: Franco is winning!
NICK: Yes, Sir.
FRANCO: Watch this.

Franco takes a puppet out of his suitcase. It is Durruti.

NICK: Who is that?
FRANCO: The anarchist bastard Durruti who thinks he's some kind of God, some kind of Franco.

Franco shoots the Durruti puppet in the neck Durruti's blood splatters all over Nick.

NICK: Jesus.

Emma speaking into a microphone.

EMMA: This is Emma Goldman reporting for Spain and The World.
Franco has bombed Madrid with German planes for three nights. Over 3,000 killed. Comrade Durruti decided to move his Column from the Aragon front to Madrid. His arrival will have a tremendous effect on the besieged workers of the city.

Lights shift. Durruti enters. Sasha's Ghost enters.

SASHA'S GHOST: Benventura Durruti.

DURRUTI: Alexander Berkman.

SASHA'S GHOST: Here is the confusing story of the day you die.

Ethyl enters.

ETHYL: On November 20th, just as Durruti is getting out of a car, a stray bullet hits him in the head, and he dies immediately.

Durruti dies. Nick enters.

NICK: No.

Durruti stands.

NICK: He is shot in the chest by a member of the communist party. He lives for hours in a coma.

Durruti dies. Dolores enters.

DOLORES: No.

Durruti stands.

DOLORES: He is shot in the neck by a fellow Anarchist. He dies a week later.

Durruti dies. Emma enters,

EMMA: No.

Durruti stands.

EMMA: Durruti is shot in the head by a fascist sniper from one of the upper stories of the Hospital Clinic.

Durruti looks at Emma.

EMMA: He dies the next day.

Durruti dies.

ETHYL, EMMA, NICK, DOLORES: Communist. Anarchist. Fascist. Neck. Head. Chest. A week, an hour, Twenty minutes, the next day.
SASHA'S GHOST: The living never do get the story right.
EMMA: His body is brought back to Barcelona.

Workers carry Durruti's body in a slow square around the stage. Soledad steps forward.

SOLEDAD: Thousands file past the open coffin. It has been arranged for
10 o'clock, but by 7, it is impossible to enter the Via Layetana. His funeral is bigger than Gaudi's'.
THE WORKERS: COMRADE DURRUTI!
EMMA: Tens of thousands raise their fists in salute.
THE WORKERS: WE SHALL AVENGE HIM! WE SHALL AVENGE HIM!
SOLEDAD: I will never forget you, My Comrade.

The Workers carry Durruti off stage.

EMMA: One more ghost, Sasha.
SASHA'S GHOST: One more ghost, Comrade.
EMMA: I can't go on.
SASHA'S GHOST: You'll go on.

Lights shift. Emma is giving a speech. Nick enters and watches her.

EMMA: Ladies and Gentlemen of Great Britain. Durruti is not dead. This great man, this thoughtful tender comrade, his great heart may beat no more, his powerful body may be felled down like a giant tree, but the fires of his flaming spirit can never be extinguished.

NICK: Miss Goldman! Nick Reynolds, Manchester Guardian. Were you in love with Durruti?

EMMA: YOU!

NICK: "Powerful body"? "flaming spirit"?

EMMA: Did you know Durruti, Mr. Reynolds?

NICK: Not personally.

EMMA: Did you see Durruti with his men and women at the front?

NICK: Can't say that I did.

EMMA: Have you been to the front?

NICK: Can't say that I have.

EMMA: THEN YOU ARE A HYPOCRITE SIR. GO TO THE SPANISH FRONT AND REPORT THE TRUTH OF WHAT YOU SEE THERE OR STAY HERE IN ENGLAND AND SHUT UP. DON'T BEMOAN THE WORLD. REBUILD IT. DON'T SEEK RESPECT. DEVELOP IT. LADIES AND GENTLEMEN, HEROISM IS SIMPLE: DO SOMETHING FOR SOMEONE. ANYTHING. A HAND, AN EAR, A WORD, A HAMMER. THAT IS THE SOLUTION. THAT IS REVOLUTION. ANARCHISM OR COMMUNISM? I DON'T CARE AS LONG AS YOU DARE TO MAKE YOUR LIFE WORTH LIVING. DIE LIVING. DIE WORKING. DIE LOVING. DIE GIVING. GIVE! GIVE! GIVE! GIVE! GIVE! AND YOU NICK REYNOLDS, MANCHESTER BLOODY GUARDIAN, GET OUT OF MY SIGHT!

Nick exits quickly. Sasha's Ghost and Lorca appear.

SASHA'S GHOST: Not sure you'll be invited to speak in Britain anytime soon.

EMMA: Where have you been?

SASHA'S GHOST: Dead.

EMMA: Don't be a smart ass.

SASHA'S GHOST: I have a lot to do. Ghosts are not fancy free, you know. It's not a Charlie Chaplain movie out here.
EMMA: So we die, and we go on working?
SASHA'S GHOST: It's been true in my case.
LORCA: And in mine. The plays keep needing rewrites. And the poems.
SASHA'S GHOST: Emma, the revolution is falling apart.
LORCA: You have to Fix it.

Franco appears holding a puppet and a machete. He looks at Emma.

EMMA: I'm going back to Spain.

Franco swings the machete and decapitates the puppet.

NICK: May 3-8, 1937
ETHYL: Fighting between CNT FAI, POUM, PSUS and police. Anarchists, Trotskyists and Communists tear each other apart.

Lights up. Barcelona. Revolutionary atmosphere has vanished. One worker runs away in fear from an Assault Guard. Another worker carries bread. It is stolen from him by another worker. Emma enters with a suitcase, watching.

WORKER ONE: Without Durruti,
WORKER TWO: The war....
WORKER FIVE: ... takes a turn
WORKER FOUR: for the worse...
WORKER FIVE: We are Hungry.
THE WORKERS: HELP US.
WORKER ONE: The enemy keeps
WORKER TWO: Pouring
WORKER FOUR: Into Spain.
THE WORKERS: Mussolini
WORKER FIVE: sends 130 aircraft

WORKER ONE: 50 whippet tanks
THE WORKERS: Hitler
WORKER FOUR: Sends 2,500
WORKER FIVE: Tons of artillery,
WORKER ONE: 500 cannons,
WORKER FIVE: 12,000 machine-guns,
THE WORKERS: H.E.-70 reconnaissance bombers He-59 floatplanes.
WORKER ONE: No one sends aid.
WORKER TWO: Only Stalin.
WORKER FOUR: And a few pistols from Mexico.
WORKER ONE: To avoid potential escalation,
WORKER FIVE: And expansion of the war,
WORKER TWO: Many countries sign an Agreement,
WORKER FOUR: Subjecting the Spanish Republic
WORKER ONE: To international isolation.
THE WORKERS: Non-Intervention.
WORKER FIVE: France closes borders with Spain.
WORKER ONE: Billboards large as buildings pierce the landscape
THE WORKERS: GET OUT OF BARCELONA! EVACUAD MADRID!
WORKER ONE :The left is split.
WORKER FOUR :Communists from anarchists, Marxists from Trotskyists
WORKER FOUR: Tearing each other apart.
WORKER ONE :Limb from limb, Heart from heart.
WORKER TWO: Brother from brother, sister from sister.
WORKER ONE: Idea from idea. Dream from dream.
WORKER FOUR: Comrade from comrade.
WORKER FIVE: The revolution is sundered into so many factions
WORKER TWO: That no one can keep them straight.
WORKER ONE: Spain is suffering
THE WORKERS :From a plague of initials:
WORKER FIVE: CEDA: Confederacion Espanola de Derechas Autonomas

WORKER ONE: CNT: Confederacion Nacional de Trabajo – anarcho-synicalist trade union
WORKER FOUR: FAI: Federacion Anarquista Iberica
WORKER TWO: POUM: The worker's party of Marxist unification
THE WORKERS: FRG GRU NKVD OVRA PCE PNV PSOE PSUC SIM UMRA
WORKER ONE: There are so many letters, of so many parties
WORKER TWO: We become confused.
WORKER FIVE: Wander into the wrong place,
WORKER FOUR: At the wrong time.
WORKER FIVE: And get ourselves
THE WORKERS: Shot.

A gunshot. Workers duck.

WORKER ONE: Where is our revolution?

Dolores enters. The Workers turn to her.

THE WORKERS: There is not enough.
WORKER ONE: Never enough.
WORKER TWO: Guns. Bread.
WORKER FIVE: Time. Bullets.
WORKER FOUR: Hope.
DOLORES: DANGER!
THE WORKERS: HELP US!
DOLORES: TO ARMS!
THE WORKERS: We are tired.
DOLORES: ARM YOURSELVES!
THE WORKERS: No arms.
DOLORES: THE FASCISTS ARE COMING!
THE WORKERS: Kill the fascists.
DOLORES: The Trotskyist Workers Party, the POU must be rooted out of the ranks of our Party as one roots out poisonous weeds.
THE WORKERS: Poisonous weeds.

DOLORES: The Trotskyists and the Anarchist must be disposed of like wild beasts.
THE WORKERS: Wild Beasts
DOLORES: FIGHT THE ANARCHIST ENEMY WITHIN!
THE WORKERS: We are the enemy…
DOLORES: DISCIPLINE, COMPOSURE, VIGILANCE!
THE WORKERS: Vigilance…
DOLORES: SAVE SPAIN!
THE WORKERS: SPAIN!
DOLORES: VIVA COMRADE STALIN!
THE WORKERS: Comrade Stalin…
DOLORES: UNITE, WORKERS OF THE WORLD!
THE WORKERS: Workers of the world…
DOLORES: TO YOUR POSTS!

The workers stagger off.

DOLORES: Welcome back to Spain, Comrade Goldman.
EMMA: You don't sound too pleased to have me back, La Pasionaria.
DOLORES: Comrade Stalin has finally wrestled the revolution away from the

Anarchists who were destroying the war effort.

EMMA: The Anarchists were guiding a thriving revolution. Comrade Durruti's column produced some of the greatest results in the war.
DOLORES: Durruti is dead.
EMMA: Why are so many of our people are under illegal arrest in Communist-controlled secret prisons?
DOLORES: The anarchists are motivated by their resentment of the centralized military command sought by the Communists.
EMMA: The Communist Party is motivated by authoritarianism to rule over all revolutionary activity.
DOLORES: Stalin is our only hope. With his directive we will win.

EMMA: More than 500 Anarchists are dead. Not by our common enemy the fascists, but by our allies the communists. Innocent men and women fighting for freedom.
DOLORES: When the life of a people is in danger it is better to convict a hundred innocent ones than to acquit a single guilty one.
EMMA: That is a dangerous view.
DOLORES: These are dangerous times. We are at war.
EMMA: A war against Franco! Not against each other! All of Northern Spain is under Nationalist control!
DOLORES: The war and the revolution are inseparable.
EMMA: If the Left turn on each other, Franco will triumph.
DOLORES: You Anarchists had your day in the sun.
EMMA: As far as I am concerned night has fallen on Spain.
DOLORES: Spanish nights are beautiful, Goldman.
EMMA: Let's just hope the dawn will eventually rise.
DOLORES: Try not to get blown up.

Lights shift. Franco enters with a suitcase. He takes out a paper model of a city and a box of matches. The workers enter.

THE WORKERS: April 26, 1937
WORKER ONE: The ancient beautiful Basque town of
THE WORKERS: GUERNICA

Franco lights the model on fire.

WORKER TWO: An aerial bombing attack
WORKER FOUR: On market day.
WORKER FIVE: 1,654 people
WORKER ONE: Killed instantly.

Franco sweeps the ashes into his suitcase. Exits. Lights shift. Orwell at the front, in a trench on the ground aiming over a hillside. Shelling. Nick appears.

NICK: Mr. Orwell?
ORWELL: Get down, BOY!
NICK: Sorry, Sir.

A stream of explosions. Nick dives into the trench on top of Orwell.

ORWELL: First time at the front?
NICK: Yes.
ORWELL: New recruit?
NICK: Nick Reynolds, Manchester Guardian.
ORWELL: Ah. Reporter
NICK: Thought I should know what it was like firsthand. Bit of hypocrisy to write about the war without coming to the front if you know what I mean.
ORWELL: Yes, well let's try not to get you killed shall we? So you'll be able to file your next article.
NICK: I read your book, Wigan Pier. I grew up near there.
ORWELL: How did you end up in Spain, Nick?
NICK: Went to Manchester. Took a journalism course. Held tight to the promise of success with the conservative press.
ORWELL: So you aren't exactly in a communist trench by way of your political ideals.
NICK: I want to be a great writer. For England.
ORWELL: Don't be a great writer for England, Son. England will never applaud you the way you dream she will. Be a great writer for your readers. And readers are from everywhere.
NICK: What will you remember most about your days at the front?
ORWELL: An old bloke singing: *"There were Rats, Rats, Rats as big as cats, in the corp, in the crop, there were lice, lice, lice as big as mice..."* Guess you could say I'll remember the music.

Orwell stands to look out over the side of a trench, a gunshot. He's hit in the neck. Nick screams. He falls back on top of Nick. His blood is streaming.

NICK: Oh dear. Oh God. Good God. Oh My.
ORWELL: Put your hands there, Son. Push down. Got to stop the bleeding.
Nick presses down with both hands on the wound.

Orwell goes limp. Nick lifts him onto his lap and keeps pushing.

NICK: Bound to be a Medic somewhere.
ORWELL: Bound to be.
NICK: Does it hurt much?
ORWELL: Not much.

Orwell passes out. Nick shakes him.

NICK: Orwell! Mr. Orwell, Sir! Please! Don't die. Sir! Please!

Orwell wakes.

ORWELL: Still here, my Boy.
NICK: Talk, then – it's important to stay awake. I read that somewhere.
ORWELL: You talk, Son.
NICK: No Sir. I'll only put you back to sleep. You must talk. Talk about anything. Talk about England.

Orwell dozes off. Nick shakes him awake.

NICK: Mr. ORWELL! SIR! SPEAK! PLEASE! SAY SOMETHING!
ORWELL: One must place six heaping teaspoons of fresh tea leaves straight into the pot, no strainer to imprison… one can swallow tea leaves of considerable quantity without any ill effect. Let the tea steep 7 minutes. No more no less. Pour the tea in the cup first – this is one of the most controversial points – one wants to precisely regulate the amount of milk. Very good tea needs no sugar. I'll have a cup of tea now, young man.

He passes out again. Nick shakes him.

NICK: Why are you in Spain, fighting for the Republic, getting shot in the neck? Dying for a country that doesn't even belong to you?

Orwell opens his eyes.

ORWELL: Common decency.

Orwell passes out again. Lights shift. Franco enters with the Hitler puppet.

FRANCO: I am sorry I am late, Herr Hitler
(as Hitler)
NO ONE IS LATE TO SEE ME!
(as himself)
I know. I am sorry. There were complications back in Spain – the anarchists-
(as Hitler)
I don't care if there were 30,000 communist troops with sabers at your throat. When you are summoned to meet me, you are punctual, or you are…
(as himself, frightened)
Are what…?
(as Hitler)
On my blacklist.

Franco exits sheepishly behind the puppet. Lights shift. A basement bar. Shelling can be heard in the near distance. Dos Passos, Dorothy Parker, Hemingway, Virginia sit at a table. A shell explodes outside.

WAITER: That's seven.
HEMINGWAY: What?
DOROTHY: He is counting the shells.

Another shell.

WAITER: Eight.
DOS PASSOS: Where the hell is Robles? He's Disappeared.
HEMINGWAY: People disappear every day.
DOS PASSOS: He is my main contact for the film.
DOROTHY: Tell him Hem.
DOS PASSOS: Tell me what?

Another shell.

WAITER: Ten.

Hemingway gets up.

HEMINGWAY: I'm going back to work.
DOS PASSOS: Sit down fool.
DOROTHY: It's too dangerous out there Hem, even for you.
HEMINGWAY: I have a chapter to finish.
DOS PASSOS: There's no work once you've been hit.

Hemingway stands. Several shells explode.

WAITER: Fifteen.

Hemingway sits back down.

VIRGINIA: Do you have any champagne?
WAITER: Champagne?
DOROTHY: Champagne? Damn it. We need whiskey.
VIRGINIA: I generally don't drink hard liquor.
DOROTHY: No I imagine hard liquor would make it difficult to walk in those tiny high heels. Especially on ancient cobbled streets dripping with blood.

A shell.

WAITER: Sixteen.
VIRGINIA: Can you please go see if you have any champagne?
HEMINGWAY: Virginia, You should marry me.
DOS PASSOS: You're already married.
HEMINGWAY: Marry me, and my wife will be our cook.
DOROTHY: You have a perfectly nice wife.
HEMINGWAY: She can cook. What do you say, Beautiful?

A shell.

WAITER: Seventeen.
VIRGINIA: I'm afraid one day you will find another girl and make me your cook.
DOROTHY: You're smarter than you look, Honey.
DOS PASSOS: What do you know about Robles?
DOROTHY: Tell him.

Several more shells.

WAITER: Twenty Four.
DOS PASSOS: TELL ME WHAT YOU KNOW!
HEMINGWAY: I've got work to do. Pay the bill, Dos and let's get out of here
DOS PASSOS: I've got no money.
HEMINGWAY: No money. No balls.
DOS PASSOS: You need to destroy our friendship every few weeks just to keep functioning.
HEMINGWAY: You arouse my inner sadist.

A huge bunch of shells.

VIRGINIA: It sounds like it's getting closer!

WAITER: Thirty seven.
VIRGINIA: Thirty eight.
WAITER: We're going to die.
VIRGINIA: GET ME SOME CHAMPAGNE!
WAITER: Lady I am really sure we don't have any.
DOS PASSOS: Hemingway!
DOROTHY: Robles was arrested.
DOS PASSOS: Shit.
VIRGINIA: You told me he was dead, Hem.
DOS PASSOS: You bastard!
HEMINGWAY: I didn't kill him!

Huge amount of shelling. Very close.

WAITER: I lost count.
DOROTHY: What makes people kill their own countrymen?
VIRGINIA: Please. Waiter. I want to die drunk.
WAITER: I don't want to die at all.
DOROTHY: Where is your family young man?
WAITER: On the front. My sisters and my brothers. All but me.
DOS PASSOS: On which side?
WAITER: Both. I have one brother and one sister that fight with the Falange for Franco and another brother and my father fighting for the Republic. My mother begged me to stay neutral.
HEMINGWAY: Your family is divided down the middle – now that's better than fiction. Imagine the dinner table.
WAITER: Sir, there is no dinner table. Not anymore. You ask What makes people kill their countrymen? I ask what makes people kill their own family?

The Waiter exits. More shelling. Emma runs into the bar. Sasha's ghost trails behind her.

DOROTHY: Emma!
EMMA: Dot!

HEMINGWAY: Emma Goldman.
EMMA: Ernest Hemingway!
HEMINGWAY: Where there is smoke there's fire.
EMMA: You don't seem titillated to see me.
HEMINGWAY: You wrote a terrible review of my last book.
DOROTHY: It wasn't terrible. She just didn't excite herself all over the page, leaving stains of adoration. You cannot abide constructive criticism.
HEMINGWAY: No one of literary import reads The Frieheit, anyway.
EMMA: Did you see La Pasionara sitting on the other side of the bar?
HEMINGWAY: She can't stand you.
EMMA: Yes, I know. I must go say hello.
VIRGINIA: Where is the waiter?
EMMA: Who is this beauty?
VIRGINIA: Virginia.
EMMA: Virginia the Virgin?
DOROTHY: Virginia the state.
EMMA: I know it well. Especially the lovely and hospitable Virginia State Penitentiary.
VIRGINIA: You were in jail?
EMMA: Oh Honey, you can't imagine how much of my life I've spent in jail.
VIRGINIA: Were you a bank robber?
EMMA: Much sexier than that, my Darling. A political prisoner.
VIRGINIA: Really?
DOROTHY: She was the "most dangerous woman in America".
VIRGINIA: Were you blowing things up?
EMMA: I was advocating free love.
HEMINGWAY: OK, Goldman that's enough.
VIRGINIA: She's telling me her story.
HEMINGWAY: She's warming up for the kill.
EMMA: What lovely eyes you have young lady, what charming lips, what a strong shoulders.

VIRGINIA: That's my thigh.
DOS PASSOS: The shelling has stopped. I am going to find out about Robles.
DOROTHY: I'll come with you. Bye, Emma. Viva la Revolution.
EMMA: Viva!

Dos and Dorothy Exit.

HEMINGWAY: What are you doing down here, Goldman?
EMMA: Heavy artillery in the streets, Friend. Sasha suggested I duck for cover.
HEMINGWAY: Sasha? Alexander Berkman? He's-
EMMA: Dead. I know. It's a long story.
HEMINGWAY: The waiter disappeared, or I'd get you a drink.
VIRGINIA: He went to find us champagne.
EMMA: What are you celebrating?
HEMINGWAY: The death of the revolution.
EMMA: The revolution isn't dying, Hem. Don't write that. She's just having a bad day.
HEMINGWAY: Come, Virginia. Let's go find you a bottle of champagne.
VIRGINIA: I don't want to go out there, Hem.
EMMA: I'll protect you, Angel.
HEMINGWAY: I'll protect her. Come on.

Hemingway pulls Virginia to her feet and drags her out. Emma enters the other side of the bar where Dolores is in a planning session with Communist Commander.

DOLORES: Goldman.
EMMA: Iburruri.
DOLORES: How are your famous American friends?
EMMA: I think they are scared and tired, but too American to admit it.
DOLORES: They think our war will make good fiction.

EMMA: Or a movie.

DOLORES: Our tragedy is their entertainment.

EMMA: They are not so callous as that.

DOLORES: What can I do for you?

EMMA: Stop killing anarchists.

DOLORES: Go back to your friends, Emma. This side of the bar is enemy territory.

EMMA: I think you choose your enemies badly. If you are going to pick a female adversary why not one of the fascists?

DOLORES: Oh believe me I have those as well. One in particular.

EMMA: Who is she?

DOLORES: Doña María del Pilar Primo de Rivera y Sáenz de Heredia, 1st Countess of the Castle of La Mota the daughter of dictator General Miguel Primo de Rivera, 2nd Marquis of Estella.

EMMA: Isn't she the president of the Sección Femenina of the Falange?

DOLORES: Yes. Franco is trying to arrange a marriage between her and Hitler to create a fascist dynasty.

EMMA: She sounds like a perfect foe.

DOLORES: She was born my foe. What is more tragic is that you were born a friend and grew into a foe. Anarchists are the enemy within.

EMMA: That's the Party line. What's yours?

DOLORES: I am the Party. I fight and die with Comrade Stalin.

EMMA: It's just you and me now, Dolores. Send your man away and tell me what you really think about me being in Spain. Woman to woman.

Dolores turns to Communist Commander.

DOLORES: Leave us.

COMMUNIST COMMANDER: Are you certain, Comrade?

EMMA: She's younger than me. In a fist fight, she'd win.

Dolores nods. He exits. Dolores leans in.

DOLORES: Various factions of the left, different nationalities, ideologies, religions have come and offered themselves to Spain. You aspired to the honor of dying for us.

EMMA: We will be comrades, then?

DOLORES: Until Franco is dead, we will support each other in the world press and hate each other behind the closed doors. But you know my heart.

EMMA: Well thank you. As I pretend to back you in public and despise you in secret, it will be good to know your heart.

DOLORES: I will say this in private and never again.

EMMA: What?

DOLORES: Thank you for coming to Spain.

Nick runs in.

NICK: Miss Goldman!

EMMA: What do you want?

NICK: Ethyl MacDonald has been arrested.

EMMA: By the fascists?

NICK: No.

Emma glares at Dolores.

DOLORES: She put the war efforts at risk with her anti-Communist diatribe.

EMMA :Thank you, Mr. Reynolds.

Emma runs out. Lights shift. Ethyl in a prison cell, coughing. Emma enters.

ETHYL: Comrade Goldman. How did you find me?

EMMA: That British reporter came to find me.

ETHYL: "Nick Reynolds, Manchester Guardian"?

EMMA: I managed to convince the prison guards I was a nurse. They said I could give you medicine.

ETHYL: Do you have any?
EMMA: Sorry.

Ethyl coughs, drinks from the bottle.

EMMA: I only have a few minutes. Tell me what happened.
ETHYL: I broadcast that an anarchist had been executed. Communist Assault Guards barged into my house. They went through every cupboard until they discovered something to hang me with – copies of your books. That was 12 days ago.
EMMA: Poor girl.
ETHYL: You've been to prison many times. I don't want to complain.
EMMA: Sometimes it seemed that Sasha and I spent more time in prison than out.

Ethyl coughs.

EMMA: What worries me more than anything is that you've been ill, and you'd be easy prey for anyone trying to make your death appear natural. Be on your guard. I'll work as quickly as possible to get you out of here.
ETHYL: Don't worry about me, Emma. Just save Spain.

Lights shift. The Front. Jason is writing a letter to his mother. Constant shelling. He ducks every time there is another shot. Viva is patching up Hermann who has been seriously injured, this time in the arm. Soledad covering them with gunfire.

HERMANN: OUCH! Be careful!
VIVA: You've made a mess of yourself this time.
HERMANN: Don't have to scrape so hard, Nurse.
VIVA: You want to die of infection? It would be a waste of the bullets we used to save you from the enemy.
SOLEDAD: Why were you running towards Franco's trench in the first place?

HERMANN: I got confused. How can you tell ours from theirs? Everything looks the same. One hole just like another.
SOLEDAD: INCOMING.

They duck. Shelling.

HERMANN: I gotta pee.

He stands.

SOLEDAD: Pee in your pants.
HERMANN: That's disgusting.

Shelling

SOLEDAD: GET DOWN, SOLDIER!
VIVA: You've been shot in the leg and the buttocks and now the arm. Next time it will be the head.
SOLEDAD: That would be a good shot.
HERMANN: You have gotten mean, Comrade.
SOLEDAD: I have woken up to the bitterness of war, Comrade. You should do the same.
VIVA: What are you writing, Jason?
JASON: Details of the war.
SOLEDAD: INCOMING!

Shelling. Everyone ducks.

JASON: I'll cover us. You rest.
SOLEDAD: When they get a little closer I'll need you. Finish your letter. Careful!

Shelling. He ducks.

VIVA: What details?

JASON: Battle stuff.
VIVA: You're going to worry her.
JASON: She'll know I am brave and not just out here wasting time, resisting the dole.
SOLEDAD: INCOMING!

Shelling. They duck

VIVA: Must be an easier way to resist the dole.

The Communist Commander enters.

COMMUNIST COMMANDER: Attention!
SOLEDAD: Attention?
COMMUNIST COMMANDER: Stand to attention, a commanding officer has arrived.
SOLEDAD: We never stood at attention with Durruti.
COMMUNIST COMMANDER: Stand at attention! Up! Up!

Everyone stands. Shelling.

SOLEDAD: CAREFUL! INCOMING!

Everyone dives back down.

COMMUNIST COMMANDER: I said STAND.
SOLEDAD: There is constant shelling. We stand to attention, we drop dead. That what you want commander? A bunch of dead soldiers on your watch?
COMMUNIST COMMANDER: What is he writing?
SOLEDAD: A letter.
JASON: Just a letter, Sir.
COMMUNIST COMMANDER: To who?
JASON: My mother.
HERMANN: Wish I could write a letter to my Mummy.

COMMUNIST COMMANDER: You are writing a letter to your mother in the middle of a battle?
SOLEDAD: Most of us have lost our parents. And our brothers. And our lovers. If he has a mother left, let him write to her!
COMMUNIST COMMANDER: You! Move to the next trench. Nearer to the enemy lines
HERMANN: Me?
VIVA: He's injured, Commander.
HERMANN: I don't know if I can fire a gun, Sir. I'm in a lot of pain.
COMMUNIST COMMANDER: If your hand works you can fire a gun. No one cares how much pain you are in. We took three casualties in that trench. We need men.
SOLEDAD: I'll go.
JASON: No I'll go.
SOLEDAD: You finish the letter to your Mama. I got nothing to lose.
VIVA: You've got a husband and three sons.
SOLEDAD: I doubt anyone on our side in Spain is still alive.
JASON: I've written enough. I'm going.
COMMUNIST COMMANDER: You are the commander of this trench, English?
JASON: Comrade Soledad is in charge.
COMMUNIST COMMANDER: Then you go. One body is as good as another.

Commander exits. Viva grabs Jason.

VIVA: Careful! Be careful.

He hands her his letter.

JASON: If I don't get back, post this to my Mum.
VIVA: It's not a Charlie Chaplain movie anymore.

He kisses Viva. He runs off.

JASON: Viva!

Gunfire. Viva covers her eyes. Lights shift.

Franco marches with his now very large suitcase. He opens it to reveal piles of dirt. He takes out several puppets larger than before, and he shoots them. As Franco shoots his puppets, lights come up on another part of the stage. Jason runs from one trench to another shooting at the enemy as he goes. Franco aims at one puppet and shoots it in the chest.

Simultaneously Jason is hit by a bullet in the chest. He falls. Dead. Lorca and Sasha's Ghost enter. Shots continue to ring out as Franco takes a small shovel out of his pockets. He buries the puppets in his suitcase, making a mass grave. Lorca and Sasha's Ghost carry Jason offstage. Lights shift.

ETHYL: 1938
NICK: March 16-18. Continuous bombing of Barcelona
ETHYL: September 21. The Prime Minister announces to the League of Nations unilateral withdrawal of all international troops.
NICK: Emma Goldman returns to Britain.

Lights shift. Emma is waiting. Nick enters..

EMMA: Nick Reynolds, Manchester Guardian.
NICK: Not many people came.
EMMA: I am not popular with the Communist party in this region.
NICK: In any region.
EMMA: What are you doing here?
NICK: Writing about you.
EMMA: Why on earth would you do that?
NICK: Because it's the right thing to do. Your audience is waiting.
EMMA: There are not even 20 people out there.

NICK: That's nearly 20 people whose minds you can change.

EMMA: You've come around.

NICK: I've come to Scotland.

EMMA: Scottish Comrades. Well…There are only a few of you here…why don't we just sit together? Pull your chairs around. That's it. I wanted to bring news of your brave countrywoman Ethyl Mac Donald. She will soon be out of prison and headed home to you. Comrades, I am not optimistic about Spain. The tide has turned against us. But what I saw there – the idealism, the cooperation, the willingness to take risks for freedom revived my faith in life. Whatever the outcome of this unequal struggle, the contribution the brave revolutionaries have made can never die and never be forgotten.

NICK: Tell us about your work there.

EMMA: My work? My work for Spain brought meager results. But it has been the greatest experience of my public life.

NICK: The Left has made a deal with Franco.

EMMA: If the International Brigade is expelled, Franco has agreed to stop receiving arms from Germany and Italy.

> *Franco enters. He bursts out laughing. Lights out on him. Lights up on Barcelona. Total ruins. The Beggar is wandering around with only one shoe waving Durruti's gun. Lights up on George Orwell in a window aiming a gun – the beggar points his gun at Orwell's bandaged neck.*

ORWELL: PUT THAT GUN AWAY.

> *The Beggar points the gun up at Orwell's window.*

BEGGAR: DON'T FIRE AT ME IF YOU FIRE ON ME I'LL FIRE ON YOU.

ORWELL: I AM NOT AIMING AT YOU. I AM AIMING AT THE BUILDING ACROSS THE STREET. PUT THE GUN DOWN.

BEGGAR: I AM ONLY A WORKER SAME AS YOU. WHY WOULD YOU WANT TO SHOOT ME?
ORWELL: I DON'T WANT TO SHOOT YOU!
BEGGAR: YOU GOT ANY BEER?
ORWELL: NO!
BEGGAR: Careful! Be careful!

Beggar exits. Franco appears behind Orwell with a puppet of Stalin.

FRANCO (AS STALIN WITH STALIN PUPPET): Comrade Orwell.

Orwell sees him and gasps.

ORWELL: Stalin!
FRANCO (AS STALIN): This assignment is making you quite insane.
ORWELL: Six days alone in a tower. With a gun trained at a hotel which is the headquarters of my own people.
FRANCO (AS STALIN): The POUM is Gestapo.

Orwell points his gun at Stalin.

ORWELL: Gestapo, Comrade Stalin? I, a middle class writer who came here to help crush fascism and got shot in the neck for the good of the working people? Look me in the eye you fat lying bastard, do I look like Gestapo?
FRANCO (AS STALIN): Spies look like everyone. And nobody.
ORWELL: Think I'm a Nazi spy, you lying power monger?
FRANCO (AS STALIN): I am not your enemy.
ORWELL: Whatever goes upon two legs is an enemy. Whatever goes upon four legs, or has wings, is a friend. No animal shall wear clothes. No animal shall sleep in a bed. No animal shall drink alcohol. No animal shall kill any other animal. All animals are equal.. but some animals are more equal than others. The pigs become more human. The humans become pigs.

FRANCO (AS STALIN): Raving mad.
ORWELL: Between the shadow and the ghost,
Between the bullet and the lie,
Where is Manuel Gonzalez,
Where is Pedro Aguilar?
Think I've gone mad? Maybe I have. Maybe I'll pull this trigger and splatter your blood all over the walls. The man that killed Stalin in Barcelona should sell a few books. But you aren't in Barcelona are you? You are in Moscow and I am in this tower of this hotel with this gun in the worst 6 days of my life.

Lights out on Orwell and Franco. Up on the street below. The Beggar points his gun at Viva and Soledad. Soledad points her rifle at him.

BEGGAR: This is Comrade Durruti's gun.
SOLEDAD: Sure it is.
BEGGAR: He gave it to me. Told Me to rob a bank.
SOLEDAD: Did you do it?
BEGGAR: I was going to do it. But then the war came.
VIVA: There are no more banks to rob.
BEGGAR: There is only hunger. Hunger and death.
SOLEDAD: Stop waving it around.
BEGGAR: It got no bullets anyway.

Soledad lowers her rifle. A cock crows. The Three of them hit the ground. A shell whistles by and explodes.

VIVA: Those cocks are good.
BEGGAR: The rabbits and the hens are better. The rabbits jump up and down like this when a bomb is coming the hens peck in little circles like this...

He imitates a pecking hen.

VIVA: Who would have known human lives could be saved by barnyard animals.
SOLEDAD: Only Lorca could have written this kind of an ending to Spain.
BEGGAR: I used to read Lorca. I prefer Shakespeare. I was a Shakespearean scholar. University of Barcelona.
SOLEDAD: That been useful for you, Comrade?
BEGGAR: Last week I traded a sliver of soap for a morsel of bread down by the pier. But this week I couldn't get anything. Except acorns.
VIVA: I've got some rationed lentils. But no way to cook them.

She empties her pockets and pours dried lentils into his hands.

BEGGAR: Lentils. They call those El Presidente's little pills. Last month I found a whole cigarette. When I had that cigarette I had the kingdom of heaven.
SOLEDAD: Don't despair, Comrade.
BEGGAR: No Senora. Nobody must despair. There is no room for Hamlet in Barcelona.

He exits.

VIVA: So are you going to find your family?
SOLEDAD There is nothing I want more than to see my husband and my children. Now I feel that nothing is as important as my family. Not even Spain.
VIVA: Be careful. The roads are not safe for us.
SOLEDAD: You have passage home?
VIVA: I traded my mother's necklace for a ticket.
SOLEDAD: You'll go to Brooklyn?
VIVA: First to London. To give Jason's letter to his mother.
SOLEDAD: Travel safely, Comrade.
VIVA: I hope that one day the revolution will be a success and Spain will be glorious again.

SOLEDAD: Con patienza y salivita se el elephante coja el'armagita.
VIVA: What does that mean?
SOLEDAD: With patience and a little saliva the elephant fucks the ant.
VIVA: Goodbye my friend.
SOLEDAD: Thank you for coming to Spain.

> *The two women hug. Viva exits. Soledad puts red lipstick on. Franco enters. He shoots Soledad dead. Lorca and Sasha's Ghost enter. They carry Soledad off stage. Lights shift. Ethyl and Nick are at a radio microphones.*

ETHYL: 1939
NICK: January 26th, Nationalists capture Barcelona. Hundreds of Americans escape to France.
ETHYL: February 27, France and Britain recognize the Franco regime.
NICK: The International brigades leave Spain. But Hitler and Mussolini continue sending in troops and weapons. Franco has gone back on his word.

> *Lights come up on Dolores.*

DOLORES: COMRADES OF THE INTERNATIONAL BRIGADES! I CAME TO SAY GOODBYE! FRANCO TOLD YOU TO LEAVE PROMISING TO STOP TAKING ARMS FROM HITLER BUT HE LIED TO YOU, HE BETRAYED US! HE FOUGHT A DIRTY WAR AND WON. HE SENDS YOU BACK. SOME OF YOU TO FORCED EXILE. GO WITH PRIDE. YOU ARE HISTORY. YOU ARE LEGEND. YOU ARE THE HEROIC EXAMPLE OF THE SOLIDARITY AND THE UNIVERSALITY OF DEMOCRACY. WE WILL NOT FORGET YOU, AND, WHEN THE OLIVE TREE OF PEACE PUTS FORTH ITS LEAVES, COME BACK TO SPAIN! VIVA!

Ethyl joins Nick at the microphone.

ETHYL: On the coldest day of the year Franco's troops march into Barcelona.
NICK: The Bourgeoise come out of hiding. And put back on their fancy hats.
ETHYL: Winston Churchill tells his countrymen:
NICK: "We have allowed our prejudice as a class to cloud our instincts as an empire"
ETHYL: April 1st. Franco declares Victory and the Spanish Civil War is over.
NICK: September 1st. Hitler invades Poland and the Second World War begins.

Franco waltzes the Hitler puppet into the sunset. Lights shift.

ORWELL: Meanwhile in England it is summer again. The milk bottles are delivered each morning. Everything is quiet and blue.

Lights shift. Emma stands with a suitcase.

NICK: 1940. Emma Goldman arrives in Canada.

Sasha's Ghost and Lorca enter.

SASHA'S GHOST: Comrade.
EMMA " It's like waiting all your life to have a child and then finally it's born only to live a few months and die young.
SASHA'S GHOST: Whenever there is WORK to do, we must be brave.
EMMA: I am frantic with worry about the Spanish orphans.
LORCA: Emma.
EMMA: What?
LORCA: Thank you for going to Spain.

Lorca exits. She looks at Sasha.

EMMA: You off again?
SASHA'S GHOST: No. This time I stay.
NICK: Goldman lectures in Toronto in both English and Yiddish. Her lectures are entitled:
EMMA: Who Betrayed Spain?

Emma crumples to the ground. Her skirt comes up. She reaches down and pulls it down over her knee.

NICK: During a speech she suffers a stroke that leaves her paralyzed on the right side. Although she regains consciousness, she never recovers the ability to speak.

Nick helps her up. Emma tries to tell him something. He gets Emma a pen and a piece of paper. Emma scrawls. He reads out loud.

NICK: "If he is a grand person I don't care what political tendencies he has." Does that mean we are finally friends?

She writes again. Hands him the paper. He reads

NICK: "The great orator is finally silenced." You'll get your voice back, Miss Goldman.
Emma writes. He reads.
NICK: "Call me Emma."

Emma writes. Nick takes the paper Emma is writing.

NICK: "Do not spend money on a tombstone. Collect funds for Spanish refugees."

Nick exits. Emma writes. Sasha takes the paper and reads:

SASHA'S GHOST: "Stay awake. Nobody must sleep! Nobody!"

Jason and Lorca and Soledad enter.

LORCA: In the sky there is nobody asleep. Nobody, nobody.
SOLEDAD: The creatures of the moon
SASHA'S GHOST: Sniff and prowl
LORCA: And bite the ones who do not dream.
SOLEDAD: The man who rushes out
JASON: With his spirit broken
LORCA: Will meet on the street corner
ALL FOUR GHOSTS: The unbelievable alligator
SASHA'S GHOST: Quiet
SOLEDAD: Beneath the tender protest of the stars.
JASON: Nobody is asleep on earth.
SASHA'S GHOST: Nobody,
SOLEDAD: Nobody.
ALL FOUR GHOSTS: Nobody sleeps.
LORCA: Life is not a dream.
SASHA: Careful!
SOLEDAD: Careful!
JASON: Careful!
ALL FOUR GHOSTS: Be Careful!
SASHA: One day
SOLEDAD: We will watch the butterflies rise from the dead.
JASON: Be careful
LORCA: Nobody is sleeping in the sky.
SASHA: Nobody,
SOLEDAD: Nobody.
LORCA: Nobody is sleeping.

Emma exits. The four ghosts follow her. Ethyl enters.

ETHYL: United States officials allowed Emma Goldman's dead body across the border to be buried in Chicago's Waldman cemetery next to the Haymarket Anarchists.

Orwell enters

ORWELL: The International Brigades included 9,000 Frenchmen, 5,000 3,000 Italians, 1,500 Czechs; 1,500 Canadians; 1,000 Hungarians and 1,000 Scandinavians. 2,800 from The United States.
ETHYL: The death toll of the International Brigades was almost 10,000.
ORWELL: Over 500,000 people died in the war. After his victory, Franco maintained a right-wing authoritarian regime through censorship, imprisonment, and forced labor. He executed over 100,000 political prisoners.
ETHYL: When he died American President Richard Nixon made a toast: "General Franco is a loyal friend and ally of / the United States."

Dolores and Durruti enter.

DOLORES: The state sanctioned reign of terror lasted until Franco's death in 1975.
DURRUTI: Barcelona finally hosted the 1992 Olympic games.
DOLORES: And the world did its best to wipe the Spanish Civil War from public memory.
ORWELL: Hardly anyone reads my book Homage to Catalonia. Few know the truth of Spain.

Nick enters

NICK: Emma Goldman once said:
DURRUTI: The Revolution in Spain
ORWELL: Has meaning for anyone
DOLORES: Who aspires to live honestly,
ETHYL: And generously
DURRUTI: And though we cannot wake the dawn
ETHYL: We can prepare the people

ALL: To greet the rising sun.

Emma enters.

EMMA: I believe in Anarchy, Freedom, Free love, Speech.
I believe in America, Courage, people, pride.
I believe there is great work to do now however we can.
Please go on believing.
In patriotism of the soul.
Our role in the liberation of humankind.
Even in these times. There are
Lines Of people all over the world, holding each other, helping each other. Protesting War. Shouting For. Freedom. Free Love. Speech. Justice. Peace. Water and air. Fair pay. The idea and the day.
Join us.
ORWELL: In Detroit.
DOLORES: London. Los Angeles.
DURRUTI: Baghdad. Paris. Hiroshima.
ETHYL: Mexico City. St. Louis. Beirut.
NICK: Barcelona. New York.
EMMA: Believe! In the spiritual, political, economic
Revolution of life. Strife! YOU and YOU and YOU.
DO WHATEVER IT TAKES TO MAKE IT HAPPEN!

Blackout.
End of Play.

www.ingramcontent.com/pod-product-compliance
Lightning Source LLC
Chambersburg PA
CBHW070149100426
42743CB00013B/2859